I place my candle in the window to those who wake up each day with shattered hearts and broken dreams. I illuminate my flame of hope for you. You are the valiant Soul Soldiers and yet still you carry on no matter how many storms you must weather. You smile and carry on. Please know that the darkest hour is always just before The Dawn. Hold on…stay strong, my friends!

To those of you who have lost loved ones to The Darkness, my candle also glows brightly for you. Take heart! For they are not gone forever. This endless night will draw to a close. They will embrace you once more in The Light and you will be happy once again.

Please keep your minds and hearts open for their messages! They still love you.

Contents

Dedication	1
A Message from Michael	5
Introduction	6
Chapter One	9
Chapter Two	15
Chapter Three	24
Chapter Four	34
Chapter Five	42
Chapter Six	48
Chapter Seven	56
Chapter Eight	66
Chapter Nine	71
Chapter Ten	80
Chapter Eleven	91
Chapter Twelve	97
Chapter Thirteen	104
Chapter Fourteen	114
Chapter Fifteen	130
Chapter Sixteen	135
Chapter Seventeen	165

Bibliography 167
Acknowledgement 169

A Message from Michael

By Rosy Baldwin

My Journey from Heartbreak to Hope

(Some names and details have been changed to protect the privacy of the individuals)

Introduction

∞∞∞

In the sultry August gloom, I stood beside my sister Jo at the East Falls Church Metro station. It was one o'clock in the morning. We were not waiting for the last subway train but were anticipating the arrival of the first participants in the "Out of the Darkness Suicide Awareness Walk." We lit our small scented candles and positioned our folding metal chairs at the station, along with scores of other supporters. All of us shared a common bond: the need to shed some light on the "heartbreak disease" of depression. Crickets chirped and spring peepers serenaded us as a few stray raindrops trickled from overcast skies. Occasional heat lightning illuminated the heavens.

Suddenly the leading walkers strode into view on the Washington & Old Dominion bike trail adjacent to the subway stop. Cheers and applause broke out as they marched down the slight hill. These dedicated people would trudge a total of twenty-six foot-blistering miles throughout Northern Virginia that late summer night before reaching the Mall in Washington, D.C. by sunrise. Some participants had photos of their departed loved ones printed on their colorful sweat-drenched tees and tank tops, close to their hearts. I myself was wearing my "Michael" tee shirt that I had created years earlier. It depicted the handsome face of my dearest friend and was designed to resemble an Old West **WANTED** poster, complete with pioneer style font lettering. Merely wearing the shirt made me feel closer to him.

Despite the oppressive humidity and the somber reason for the event, all of the marchers were friendly and smiling. My heart longed to ease their pain, to support their courage. While talking to some of them, I discovered that several had lost their loved ones to suicide only months before. The wounds were still jagged, raw. Overcome with bittersweet emotion, I whistled and cheered along with the rest of the crowd, lifting my flickering candle high! Some compassionate souls next to us were providing fresh, cool watermelon slices and flavored ice pops for the tired and thirsty walkers, who numbered in the thousands. Jo and I left the station around 3:30 that long ago morning when the last foot soldier passed by, waving at us. It was a powerful experience. I was glad that my sister and I had been a part of the marathon, if only as bystanders.

The statistics on suicides are disturbing: 30,000 souls in the United States *alone* take their own lives each year. Hundreds of thousands more attempt suicide and don't succeed...at that time. Depression is increasingly being recognized for what it is, a serious mental illness that should carry no disgrace, no finger-pointing. Millions of people will suffer from it during some period of their lives. *Nobody is guaranteed immunity from this disorder; it is oblivious to race, sex, religion, economic status or education.* It strikes especially hard at our young people and it re-emerges as a potent force in our twilight years as well. Throughout history, some of humankind's finest and brightest have fallen dark and silent from this affliction.

A Message from Michael is really threefold in purpose. First, I am trying in a very modest way to shed some light on depressive illness, at least from the viewpoint of what I observed in my friend Michael. The second purpose is to present the reader with a quick artist's sketch of someone whose passing made this world a less vibrant and less caring place. Although I didn't know Michael long, he touched my life as no other person who has crossed my path. I feel honored to have met such a generous, loving, and intelligent man. When he departed this life by his own hand, tremendous sorrow followed in his wake. Finally,

I wanted to share my own experiences with what I believe is Michael's spirit in the afterlife. I'm happy to say that he hasn't changed much from the person I came to know and love.

Perhaps the last reason is the most important one of all; he lives on…

Like many overbusy people whose modern lives are filled with a thousand mundane obligations and worries, I rarely have a quiet moment to just sit and contemplate, let alone write. Yet for some reason, the thoughts in this book seemed to flow freely. Tears often ran down my face but an occasional smile also flickered across my countenance as I typed this story.

I'd like to think that Michael was at my side helping me write it. It comes from my heart. May you find some comfort in my words.

Rosy Baldwin
(Originally Written October 2003)
Revised August 2020

Chapter One

Promise

I awoke with a start. Raindrops were falling gently outside my open bedroom window that October morning. A faint breeze fluttered the sheer curtains. The sky was autumn gray, somber. I reached for my digital watch: 7:00 on the dot. I shivered slightly as an unexpected whisper of melancholy passed over me. But within minutes, a watery, lemon-tinted sun broke through the clouds and soon the world was painted with a joyful palette of reds, oranges and golden hues as the clouds departed. It promised to be an exquisite fall day: One of those crisp blue, sun-kissed sky days that is like a shiny surprise gift waiting to be unwrapped and treasured. It was the sort of day that brings to mind clean white laundry, snapping and dancing briskly on a clothesline, smelling faintly sweet and sunny warm.

It was a day like no other.

On October 10, 1997 I was utterly in love and my love was returned in full by a man named Michael Hardesty. Only seven hours earlier, at midnight, Michael and I had spoken on the phone. He had confessed several times, "Oh, Rosy, I love you so much honey! I want us to share the rest of our days together. I want it more than anything in the world, anything." he said. "But I don't think you want it as much as I do. Don't you want to go for the 'brass ring,' Rosy?" Of course I did and I told him so. I had never been married before nor had I ever lived with anyone. At times I felt hopelessly old-fashioned, a Victorian heart in a modern world. I had dated a few men over the years but they had either burned me badly or we didn't seem compatible for the long haul. I was on the brink of abandoning my quest for a true life's companion when I met Mike. His words that evening were the lyrics to a joyful melody composed for my lonely soul. The man of my dreams was speaking the sentences I had waited a lifetime to hear! Life seemed good again and it felt oh so wonderful to walk in the sunshine once more.

Unlike any previous time in our relationship, we had spoken at least half a dozen times on October 9th. I was slightly puzzled by Michael's numerous phone calls but nonetheless was happy to hear from him. After his romantic declarations, our midnight conversation had ended on a rather mundane note with my boyfriend saying, "Well, I better try and get some sleep now. I feel kind of hungry. I think I'll go downstairs and eat a hefty bowl of Raisin Bran! Are you going to be up for awhile, sweetie? I might want to call you later. After all, don't forget that you're my 'night nurse!'" he joked.

"Yeah, the Raisin Bran sounds good. Maybe I'll eat some too! I'll probably go to bed earlier tonight Mike. It's been a long day for me, with Winky (my pet mouse) dying and all. But you can call if you want. I might be up."

"Oh that's right! Winky, your poor little mouse. You had a funeral for him in the back yard this afternoon, didn't you? Rosy and her mice!" he laughed softly, "Well, just imagine the two of us together, walking hand in hand through the snow that'll fall this winter, and please call me in the morning? Will you do that for me? Please call me. Love you."

"Love you too, Mike. Sleep well, honey. I'll call you in the morning." I smiled as I hung up the phone. Michael always looked forward to his nightly cereal snacks.

As I lay in bed that sunrise, those delightful snippets of conversation cavorted through my mind, playful kittens of reverie. Another reassuring sentence replayed in an endless loop: Mike proclaiming, "You know Rosy, I think I'm finally beginning to see the light at the end of the tunnel!"

Indeed, this affirmation was heartwarming, as he had been suffering at the time from a sudden, inexplicable sadness that had hit him in mid July and had gathered momentum like an angry thunderstorm during August and September. He had visited the Fairfax Hospital (Virginia) ER numerous times with severe panic attacks and had seen several doctors. They had prescribed an arsenal of medications, including Paxil, Restoril, Ambien, Clonopin, Flexeril and Ativan in an attempt to alleviate his growing sleeplessness, melancholy, body aches and anxiety attacks. Walking had always been enjoyable for him but even this simple exercise caused him chest pain when he took a stroll around the block. His cardiologist could find no abnormalities on his EKG, however. Michael had never experienced such a baffling array of symptoms before and he was growing frantic attempting to solve the puzzle of what was ruthlessly attacking his spirit, mind and body.

Mike had always been quite healthy, lithe and fit from lifting weights and walking. He could play a mean game of basketball and was an excellent swimmer. He moved with a catlike grace that belied his age. His dietary weaknesses included generous slices of elaborately frosted birthday cake, rich strawberry shakes, bacon cheeseburgers from Roy Rogers, and his beloved Mickey's Malt Ale, with that wise-ass little cartoon bee on the bottle cap. Nonetheless, this diet seemed to cause no ill effects. I noted that he often had a ripe banana, apple or pear sitting on the counter in his shop to supplement his lunch. Sometimes he had all three fruits arranged in a tidy row, in true Virgo fashion.

He was a small man, around five foot five, but he always carried himself with dignity, with coolness. T-shirts, tight jeans, leather vests and Western hats formed his usual wardrobe, but he had been known to don various old military uniforms or funky headgear and appear in public dressed that way. His close friends told me that years before I met him, he'd arrive at his bookstore attired as legendary train engineer Casey Jones, complete with bib overalls, striped railroad cap and gold pocket watch! A vanity plate on his old Mercury station wagon even read "KCJONES."

Whimsy and imagination were facets of Michael's personality that I could relate to since I was a graphic artist, and I relied on those same qualities in my creative endeavors.

Michael was an extremely bright, articulate and thoughtful person who had lived on the earth fifty-three years when we met. He seemed much younger, with his boyish dark looks, penetrating brown eyes and razor sharp Iowa wit. His normal voice sounded much like actor William Hurt's. He displayed an uncanny talent for imitating John Wayne, Clint Eastwood, Johnny Cash, James Mason, Count Dracula or his grandma Mabel who had raised and adopted him as a little boy. His vocal mannerisms never failed to bring a grin to my face.

He owned a small antiquarian bookstore located on bustling Columbia Pike in Bailey's Crossroads, Virginia. Besides selling rare books, he also peddled vintage record albums, 45's, and a few antiques. His bread and butter money, however, came from repairing TV sets and VCRs. Mike was a soul thirsty for knowledge and reading was his passion. To him, the beautifully bound, musty-smelling volumes were dear old friends and he treated each one he possessed as gently as one would a delicate baby bird in hand. His inquisitive mind gravitated toward the philosophical works of Arthur Schopenhauer and Friedrich Nietzsche. Volumes of Herman Melville, Charles Dickens, Ayn Rand, Voltaire, Guy de Maupaissant, Oscar Wilde, and Ernest Hemingway occupied his little shop and filled his life. History books, military memoirs, fine art collections and heavy coffee-table volumes brimming with faded photographs of bygone days delighted him as well.

Trains and railroads never failed to captivate him. I was the same way. At some point in our lives, we had both owned model trains and had created layouts complete with tiny electric lights, bridges, buildings, trees, people and animals. Mike often created his own trackside structures from scratch. Plastic prefabricated model kits constructed with the over-zealous use of airplane glue were more my specialty. We felt a sense of control over a world in miniature, I suppose. One could engineer train wrecks and derailments and nobody ever got hurt. Toy choo-

choos brought out the "Christmas morning kid" in a person. In some ways, Michael and I were like Peter Pan and Wendy. We had no intention of ever really "growing up!"

Both of us were parents to much-pampered felines. He had two female kitties named Squeeky and Magic. Squeeky was a fifteen-year-old brownish tabby and full of mischief despite her advanced age. She obviously adored Michael and followed him everywhere and slept on his chest at night. Appetizers left unattended on the table were never safe as she would steal them and carry them off in her mouth to consume elsewhere in peace. Michael played his music LOUD and Squeeky would dart hither and yon, streaking up and down the stairs when he listened to his record collection. Magic was a beautiful, dainty cream-colored Manx with saucy ways. With her high rump and lack of a tail she reminded me of an adorable little bunny. I had three cats of my own named Sir Winston, Cassie and Snuggles.

Music played a major part in our lives, Michael with his guitar and I with my electronic keyboard. Frequently in his bookstore we would hold jam sessions. We turned up the amp, playing and howling away into the microphone, no doubt causing many customers to wonder exactly what kind of business Mike operated! He tried to teach me guitar but I didn't seem to have the hands for it; my fingers could barely stretch across the fingerboard as I attempted to play chords. I decided to stick to my Yamaha. I loved watching him play, however. He really came alive with a guitar in his hands. Upon hearing a song once or twice, he was able to pick up the tune and play it note for note. His tastes in music ran the gamut from classical Rossini to the Kingston Trio to AC/DC. He had a soft spot for Johnny Mathis, Buddy Holly and Elvis.

We had been seeing each other since January of that year but already our bond seemed as old as time itself. I felt kinship with him as I have never felt with any other human being before or since. He often said he felt the same way about me. Twin souls we seemed to be: one spirit joined at the heart. Many times we finished each other's sentences, and we laughed at the same things, had the same dark and unusual sense of humor. Meaningful coincidences became the cornerstone of our relationship.

But I return to October 10, 1997. That crisp, golden delicious apple morning filled with shimmering hopes and rainbow dreams promised to open an exhilarating new chapter in my life. There was no foreshadowing that by day's end, I would find myself stumbling blindly on a path marked "Dark Night of the Soul."

Chapter Two

Unanswered Call

The previous evening on the phone I had promised Michael that I would call him in the morning, giving him the green light for our plans to move in together. We both felt that this would be best since his two adult daughters, Robin and Monica, were not able to easily leave their young families and move in with their father at that juncture. I think Mike's sudden illness overwhelmed them because they had always looked up to their Dad as a helpful, independent and stalwart Rock of Gibraltar. He adored his girls and his six grandchildren and he proudly displayed their family portraits at his bookstore. Now, the parent-child roles were dramatically reversed.

Mike understood that I needed to tell my father about our plans; after all I still lived in his house, along with my older sister Jo and my mother Anne. Jo and I have always been very close, almost like twins and we shared care-giving duties for my mother. My seventy-two year old mom was completely bedridden and helpless with devastating multiple sclerosis. Mentally she seemed just as shackled. I had decided on moving in with Mike but was determined not to shirk my duties to Mom at the same time. It was wearisome work caring for her. Despite home health aides and nurses assisting us several days a week, the job was too much for either Jo or me to perform alone. There were no vacations, no days off, *ever*. Some harried, hurried days we barely squeezed an hour of free time into our schedules. (Sadly, Mom has since passed on to a far better world, December 5,

2004. May her beautiful soul dance to the music she always loved so much!)

The term "emotional burnout" is a major understatement to describe one's state of mind going through such an ordeal. You grow exhausted down to your very soul. And it was disheartening to see Mom sliding downhill from the vivacious woman she used to be. Before the disease had progressed, she had taken an active interest in the National Symphony Orchestra and had attended weekly concerts at the John F. Kennedy Center for the Performing Arts and The Friday Morning Music Club in downtown Washington, D.C. She had played the violin, piano and accordion earlier in her life. All of this was lost to her as her mind and body both slipped into a twilight world.

I felt empathy for my sister, staying behind in our family home while I forged a new life with Michael. She seemed quite unhappy about it too but she understood that I loved him deeply and wanted to help him win his ongoing battle with depression. Guilt over leaving her behind nibbled away mouse bites of my happiness.

Around 9:20 that morning I mustered my courage and I told Dad about our plans, expecting some major static. But he seemed surprisingly resigned to it, grumbling, "Well you *are* an adult after all and it's *your* life. I suppose you won't be around to look after your mother or balance the family checkbook now!" I reassured him that I would and I walked over to the wall phone in our den to call Michael. This was the same phone over which the two of us had spoken only hours earlier, planning our happy future. Before placing the call, I glanced at the blue-green numerals displayed on the VCR: 9:28 a.m.

I cannot explain this, but for some peculiar reason, after the very first ring to Michael's house, I knew that something was horribly wrong. The phone rang and rang and rang but nobody picked it up. I reasoned that he must be on his way to open Mike's Books, so I waited a few minutes and dialed that number. There was no answer.

Thus began my frantic attempts to contact him, first at

home, then at his bookstore, then at home, and then again at his bookstore: a dizzying series of calls that I placed to both locations. I lost count of the number of times I tried. Within an hour fear began to grip me, forming a visceral, hard knot in the pit of my stomach. My palms grew sweaty and my heart started beating like an erratic, crazy drum. Jo tried to calm me down, telling me that he was most likely driving around in his station wagon, enjoying the gorgeous Indian summer day. I responded, "I don't think so! He's probably lying in a pool of blood, and the phone's ringing on his nightstand over and over again, shrill as a banshee!!" She just laughed and brushed that idea aside as nonsense. Nonetheless, that was the gruesome vision that kept projecting on the screen of my worried and increasingly hysterical mind.

As the day wore on and my calls to him proved fruitless, I grew more desperate and I tried to reassure myself with what Jo was telling me. I took deep breaths and attempted to calm my fears and dread. Around eleven o'clock, we decided to visit Long Branch Nature Center, not far from Michael's shop. Walking was a great way to release tension. We would check on his bookstore after we walked a bit. We would be calm and rational and enjoy this God-given day. *Nothing really awful could happen on such a beautiful morning.* First we went inside the rustic nature center building to see the exhibits of stuffed wild animals. I recall a raccoon and a beaver looking eerily lifelike, staring at us with their beady glass eyes. Turtles played and basked in an indoor pond with a rippling waterfall. I grew claustrophobic inside the small structure and we were soon out in the open air again. We had ambled about halfway down a steep nature trail; colorful leaves were scattered on the still-damp asphalt beneath our feet. From out of nowhere, I was jolted with a sudden shocking sensation.

Michael was walking between Jo and me!

I could feel his presence to my left, matching me stride for stride. Never in my life have I had such conviction. I *knew* he was there, unbelievably sad and trying to comfort us. It was as if he were saying, "Sorry Rosy. The plans we made are off. I couldn't go through with them, honey. I just couldn't hold on any longer. I want you to know I'm still with you though. Always with you." I didn't actually see or hear anything, but I felt his strong presence and it scared me. It could mean only one thing—*that Michael was dead.* The feeling grew even more powerful as we wended our way down to bubbling Four Mile Run stream and sat on a bench beside the water. By now I was truly terrified. The world seemed too bright, garish...mocking me with its autumnal perfection.

(Years later I would feel similar mixed emotions as I watched the Pentagon and Twin Towers burning on another gorgeous day, September 11, 2001.)

My sister and I left Long Branch and drove past Mike's shop, and my last trembling butterfly of hope perished. His store was locked, drapes pulled tightly across the front window, no station wagon parked out front in its accustomed space. The blue and white clock sign on his door proclaimed "Closed. Will Return at 10." We checked the Salvation Army on Little River Turnpike, where he often shopped, but he was not there. I tried to call him several more times from the pay phone outside of Safeway at Bailey's Crossroads Center, all to no avail. I dialed his friend Marion's number over and over again. She never answered either. For a second time that morning, Jo and I toyed with the idea of driving ten miles to Mike's home in Fairfax, but some unspoken feeling stopped us. *I will always be grateful for that gut instinct.* Both times I steered the car in that direction, a picture of Mike's silent house, his car parked outside, flashed in my mind. I did not want to face that house; something ghastly was out there. At that point, despite reassurance from Jo, I knew it. I turned my car back toward Arlington.

The rest of the afternoon was a feverish kaleidoscope of buying groceries at Westover Market, eating McDonald's fish fillet sandwiches, dealing with my mom's nurse Peggy who was sure "everything was going to be just fine with Mike" and trying to call Mike, his daughter Monica or Marion. I was getting nowhere and was sick with panic.

The minutes ticked by agonizingly slow, each one adding more dread to my heart. Around two o'clock, I finally reached Mike's mother Miriam. She and I liked each other and Michael had strongly encouraged us to be friends. She seemed unconcerned about him, seemed to think he was OK; he had lots of things planned for that day. She told me to calm down. It wasn't clear to me whether she had actually talked to him earlier or she was assuming these things. For the first time that long day I felt a shower of relief wash over me, a soothing balm. I quit calling Michael's house and his bookstore. I even started feeling rather foolish, like Chicken Little with the sky falling. Of *course* he was just fine! I had a wild imagination. He must be out running errands or enjoying a much-deserved day off. *Perhaps he was so thrilled about my moving in with him he was celebrating!* Somehow all these thoughts rang false and hollow in my heart.

By the time the clock showed five fifteen, I was on the verge of calling the police or the local hospitals to locate Michael. He was always a reliable man and I knew it was completely out of character for him not to contact me, especially after our conversation the previous night. At this point I was 100% convinced that something was very much amiss and so was Jo. On the same beige den phone, I finally reached his younger daughter Monica at home. When she answered the phone, it sounded as if she had been crying.

I identified myself and she said, "Oh Rosy. I am *so* sorry!"

I asked, "*What? What is it?*"

She pronounced the words that I will never forget, words branded into my soul.

"Dad shot himself this morning."

Jo was sitting in the den. She heard me scream, **"Oh my God, no! Don't tell me that! Don't tell me that!"** as I collapsed into a spasm of sobs. It was too horrid for words, too black to see and I could not breathe. I felt like I had been hit full force with a locomotive and yet was somehow still alive, dazed and wretched. Jo guessed right away what I had heard and she turned deadly pale. "Oh God! He's **DEAD!** *Joey, Mike's dead!* He shot himself. I can't stand it. Oh God what am I gonna do?" I wailed endlessly in pure anguish.

I ran out to the front yard where Dad was sitting in a lawn chair and I choked out the news. He was stunned, and kept repeating, "Oh Christ, I'm so sorry. I'm so sorry. Oh poor Mike, poor son of a bitch. He was so sick, so very sick!" It wouldn't have done any good to tell Mom, as her mind was already gone. She had met Michael a few times; he had serenaded her on her birthday with his guitar the previous May Day, but she would not remember him. So I didn't tell her.

As the hours dragged funereally on, the hours of the promising golden day, more news trickled in. According to one of Michael's friends who had the grisly task of identifying his body for the Fairfax County police, he had shot himself in the head with a shotgun around 8:30 that morning. This had taken place in Michael's bedroom and there was simply no head left. It was too nightmarish to contemplate—beautiful Michael so maimed and ruined! To never look into those soft, wise brown eyes again. If I had owned a gun on that desolate night, I would have followed him into the dark.

This was not his first suicide attempt either; he had held a pistol to his head at 8:30 in the morning three weeks earlier and had called 911. The paramedics had arrived at his home in the nick of time. After being evaluated at Woodburn Mental Health Center, Mike was escorted by police to Alexandria's Mount Vernon Hospital where he stayed only four days before he released himself against medical advice. He had never been a patient in a hospital before and he hated it. He didn't feel he was getting the treatment he needed. I had been aware of this attempt since he had left several desperate phone messages for me while I was out buying Mom some medical supplies at the Bailey's Crossroads CVS convalescent equipment store. Strange as it seems today, back in 1997 nobody had cell phones. Answering machines and pay telephones were the standard of the day. By the time I was able to reach him, he had already been admitted to the facility. For some reason I was not permitted to visit him there. Only his family was welcome. I was very frustrated and miserable being shut out of his life in that manner.

Jo and I called Michael at the hospital on the morning of Saturday, September 20th to wish him a happy 55th birthday. We asked him point blank if he had any more guns at the house or anywhere else. He reassured us that he did not. Fairfax County police had confiscated the pistol. We sighed in relief, assuming that the officers dispatched to his house had removed any other weapons he might own. A *big* worry was laid to rest. Later that day, I learned from Marion that he had checked himself out of Mount Vernon, and my worries began to flock around me again, like raucous, unruly seagulls. I knew he couldn't *possibly* be cured in only four days!

When he came out he seemed different, aloof. I think the doctors had advised him to straighten out his own life and not to focus on romantic entanglements he might have. It hurt me but I bit my tongue and tried to be supportive of him without being smothering. I wanted him to know I cared deeply but I didn't want to appear too needy or dependent. I told him I would not call him every day like I had in the past, but would wait for him to phone me. It was a very difficult tightrope to walk, to balance. To add further turmoil to this time, I had heard a rumor that Mike might be seeing an old girlfriend again. I didn't know what to think, what to believe. I was sick with doubt, worry and unhappiness.

I checked out numerous books about depression and insomnia from the Arlington County Library, attempting to understand the horror devouring our lives. I lent most of them to Mike as well. One slim volume I noticed at the library but did not check out was *Darkness Visible* by William Styron, author of the acclaimed *Sophie's Choice*. To this day I regret that I didn't read that autobiographical account and share it with Michael. When I perused that powerful little book at a later date, I was stunned by how similar Mr. Styron's ordeal was to Michael's.

But September wound down and it seemed he was improving with his new medications, especially the Paxil. He became more industrious, bursting with ideas about improving his business, which had been sluggish all summer. He grew closer to me once again and things began to look up.

That is, until Squeeky died.

Michael took Squeeky's death *very* hard. She was his faithful companion and they had written many chapters in life's book together. I was told that he was frantic with worry years before when she went missing for several weeks. He was ecstatic when she finally reappeared at his door rail thin but otherwise okay after being trapped in a neighbor's shed all that time.

I can still see Squeeky in my mind's eye, the night she lay dying on his tiled bathroom floor. She was motionless, her eyes staring, sides heaving with shallow breaths, but occasionally she pawed the air with all four tiger-striped legs. Michael had put a soft old towel over her delicate kitty body as he tenderly tried to administer warm milk to her, using a blue ear syringe. She weakly lapped a bit of it but one stray drop fell from the syringe and landed on her dainty pussy willow front paw. It lay there glistening like a single white pearl and somehow it was heartbreaking. Her tiny body labored so hard to live. She even managed a feeble purr. Only a few days earlier she had seemed fine, galloping around the house like a little striped pony, with her bright green eyes and sassy ways. Mike kept going into the bathroom every few minutes to check on her. Tears were streaming down his face and mine both. She was truly his child. When she died, I think part of him went with her. I was told he buried "Squeeks" in his backyard the following Sunday during a torrential rain.

Only after Mike's death did I learn that he had half-heartedly attempted a second suicide, a desultory scratch to his arm using a razor blade. It was all too mind-boggling to assimilate. He had also abruptly quit drinking near the time the depression kicked in and I always suspected that his sudden abstinence might have been a factor in the disease's onset. Although Michael was diminutive, he could knock back quite a few from time to time. By midsummer, he no longer took pleasure in drinking any alcohol, as it seemed to provoke uncomfortable and alarming symptoms when he imbibed. Even his favorite Mickey's malt ale had this effect on him. So he gave it up, cold turkey.

But to my naive eyes, by early October he appeared to be improving and during our midnight talk on the phone there was no indication whatsoever that he was going to end his earthly days forever some eight hours later. Michael sounded truly optimistic. And he hadn't even waited for my call that morning...

Chapter Three

Goodbye for Now

The summer I was fifteen I watched *Love Story* in the cool and comfortable Springfield Cinema, with its "rocking chair" seats. Much of the movie is set during a New England winter and the final scenes take place near Christmas. I can recall the contrast between that scorching 1971 day and the snow-filled images on the film. I can also remember my eyes brimming with tears during the last scene where Oliver sits forlornly on the bleachers at the Central Park skating rink. Only a heartbeat ago, he and his wife Jenny were skating and laughing at the park, sipping hot cocoa to ward off the December chill. But now she is gone. She has just died in a nearby hospital. To outward appearances, everything looks precisely as it did twenty-four hours earlier. Everyone goes about his or her daily business exactly as before…but the one you love, the one your heart longs for is gone forever. No matter where you go on this planet, you will *never* be able to talk to this person again, to touch them or to embrace them.

The Grim Reaper has tapped his bony hand on your shoulder.

If possible, October 11, 1997 was even more beautiful weather-wise than the previous day. Our British friend Ed came over that Saturday and he coaxed Jo and me into taking a long trek through Bluemont Park, located on the Washington & Old Dominion bike trail. I was very reluctant to go as I felt miserable and my eyes were swollen, my face blotchy red from crying all night. I had a headache too. We walked quite a bit, pausing by Four Mile Run stream to gaze at the tiny silvery minnows swimming in the shallow water. The sky was pure cerulean blue and the families with their noisy kids, strollers, dogs and Frisbees were everywhere, laughing and running, playing touch football and softball. Couples sauntered by hand in hand. The smell of charcoal briquettes wafting from many grills was in the air. Every face I saw was smiling. I felt a banished outcast from the human race. I worried about Mike's soul, whether he had gone to Hell or Purgatory for taking his own life. I could not bear to think of him suffering further in some lost world or black starless vortex. Mike's Books, Records & TV Repair was only blocks away and I had an impulse to stop by and stare at his locked door and cry enough tears to drown myself.

After our walk we ate lunch at Shoney's in Falls Church. The entire restaurant was filled with happy twosomes, looking soulfully into each other's eyes. Some appeared to be newlyweds while others were comfortable older couples, still very much in love after many seasons together. I felt physically ill with envy, loss and anger. I couldn't help it. I felt so cheated! Life was so unfair! I barely choked down a few bites of my burger.

We went home and Ed was doing his best to cheer up Jo and me. But when he played a cassette he had brought over, and he and Jo began to dance a vigorous polka step, laughing and thumping merrily about the basement floor, I lost it.

I screamed, "Oh God, stop it! *I can't stand any more of this stupid shit!* You're *horrible people!* Why don't you just leave me alone? *Go the hell home, Ed!"* I burst into tears and ran upstairs. They felt very bad about it and apologized but the entire day was a nightmare.

The next hurdle looming ahead was the funeral. Michael died on a Friday but would not be buried until the following Thursday, pending his autopsy. A graveside service at Quantico National Cemetery was scheduled for Michael at noon sharp. I wasn't sure I would be able to attend. I wanted to be at the ceremony, to show him my love and support, but I didn't know if I could bear it. But I was determined to at least *try*. He deserved that much, surely.

Jo insisted on accompanying me that overcast, chilly Thursday. I think she feared I might have plans to park my car along the highway and jump into the Potomac River on the way to the funeral! Perhaps I did toy with that idea. I know that the long forty-four mile drive down old Route One on October 16th seemed like a surreal dream to me.

I chose Route One over the faster Interstate 95 because I got quite nervous on freeways. It was part of an ongoing anxiety disorder that I had suffered from for years. I didn't feel comfortable in crowds, large buildings or driving too far away from my home. Michael had known all about this problem and he had been very empathetic about it, never critical. However he did begin to wonder whether his own growing anxiety might not be feeding off mine somehow. It was a sobering thought.

Route One or Jefferson Davis Highway as it was previously named, is a main drag originally built in the late 1920's. The Virginia portion of it starts in Old Town Alexandria and winds its way south, roughly paralleling 95 on the right and the railroad and Potomac River on the left. The highway has been developed quite a bit over the past two decades with numerous fast food joints, townhouses, apartments and strip shopping malls. But it still has many of the familiar old used car lots, motor courts, mom and pop restaurants, gas stations and derelict rusty signs that I remembered from my childhood when we traveled that route to visit my grandparents in southern Virginia. I kept experiencing an eerie sense of déjà vu the closer we came to the burial grounds.

As I drove my car in the direction of the National Cemetery located next to the Marine base and FBI headquarters at Quantico, I began to realize that something quite unusual was happening to both Jo and me. Even though we were incredibly morose, we noticed that neither one of us was experiencing any of our usual panic or anxiety. We even made an anemic joke about Michael's spirit riding along with us, helping us cope. I patted the parking brake between the front seats and said, "It's not very comfortable for you there, is it Mike? Why don't you sit in the *back* seat for awhile?" At the point Jo and I were expressing this gallows humor, something distracted my attention over to my left.

The former Richmond, Fredericksburg & Potomac railroad tracks passed over an antiquated bridge span at that location, where the Occoquan River flowed near the towns of Occoquan and Woodbridge. A long, slow freight train was winding its way over the truss bridge. A single beam of sunlight pierced the clouds just then, making a brilliant spotlight from the heavens shining down on the train and causing the water to sparkle like diamonds. It was breathtaking but it was far more than that.

The hair on the back of my neck stood up. Several years earlier I had experienced an unusually lucid dream. In that dream ***I was looking at a railroad bridge with a freight train lumbering across it. The span was crossing the water, which was shimmering with a lone shaft of sunlight piercing a dreary overcast sky!*** What I observed outside my driver's side window was identical in every detail to my dream.

At the time in my life when the dream had occurred, I hadn't met Michael and had no reason to think I would be traveling anywhere near railroad tracks since none are near my home in North Arlington. I also recall the nightmare disturbing me for days, as the accompanying mood of it had been extremely melancholy.

As if that weren't eerie enough, Michael had told me of a dream *he* had had the previous spring. In his nighttime experience, he was living in the little town of *Quantico, Virginia.* He and I were walking through the town together in the spring sunshine. After this dream he also claimed to recall quite vividly the topography of the town: where the church, stores, post office, town square and railroad were located. He saw this layout from a bird's-eye point of view, as if he were floating over the town. He observed it so clearly that he said he could have sketched it on paper. Today, he resides there.

We arrived at the funeral service a few minutes past twelve but luckily it had not started yet. About two dozen people were there, mostly family, a smattering of Mike's bookstore friends and his next door neighbors. Marion was there with her daughter Toni and granddaughter Lee. She gave me a warm hug. Mike's brother Tom traveled over a thousand miles from their hometown of Sigourney, Iowa, accompanied by his pretty opera singer daughter, Tamara. Jo and I had ordered an arrangement of white roses the previous day and we noted with relief that it had arrived on time. For some reason I was expecting a casket and felt mild shock when I saw the military officials bearing an elegant urn holding Michael's ashes in addition to an American flag commemorating his four years of service in the United States Navy.

Monica, Tom and Mike's friend Mel spoke briefly. Monica read some excerpts from Michael's journal. Mel gave a eulogy and Tom read a touching poem about his Little Brother. Then Tamara closed the ceremony by singing Franz Schubert's hauntingly sublime "Ave Maria" in her angelic soprano voice. That's when my tears began to cascade in earnest. To this day I cannot hear that musical masterpiece without getting misty-eyed. The funeral was quite brief and when it was over, everyone scattered like autumn leaves blown by a chilly wind, and they drove off their separate ways.

I felt limp with relief that I had attended but I also felt numb and dreary. Michael was really gone. I had seen the pretty little vase of ashes and the sad faces of those who loved him. The drive back home seemed endless.

"Experts" say the grieving process has several stages starting with shock, disbelief, and numbness. Midway through the mending of your broken heart you might feel denial, sadness, and anger. Finally one is supposed to attain acceptance and healing. Coping with loss is a very personal thing and no one has the right to dictate how long it is "supposed to" take. Sometimes it seems you are moving forward in life with great strides only to feel unbearable sadness on anniversaries, birthdays or holidays.

In the case of suicides, anger often manifests itself. One

feels anger at the injustice of it all, anger and regret directed at yourself and at others for things that might have been done differently and anger at the departed loved one for leaving you so abruptly. On the one hand you can empathize with the unbearable agony that caused the suicidal person to commit that final act. On the other hand, it still feels like a rude, stinging slap in the face. *I don't think anybody wants to die.* I think they simply want to feel better and get on with their lives once again. Suicide is the permanent solution to what usually is a temporary problem, but the heartsick victim cannot see that, blinded as he or she is by pain and darkness.

The days immediately following a death are crucial for survivors, because they are at a heightened risk of suicide themselves. It seems the old story of Romeo and Juliet is not far off the mark. Anyone who has experienced the loss of a dear one will tell you, it truly feels like your soul is ripped asunder and half of it is left to die out in the howling Siberian wasteland of winter.

In an abstract, philosophical way I believed in an afterlife. Over the years I had read a number of books on the subject. Born under the sign of Neptune-ruled Pisces, I had a natural metaphysical bent. I studied books by Ruth Montgomery, Arthur Ford, Edgar Cayce, Dr. Raymond Moody, Jess Stearn, Hans Holzer and Jeanne Dixon. During that time I came across a publication authored by Patricia Romanowski and Joel Martin about psychic medium George Anderson. I read with fascination about how Mr. Anderson appeared to contact dead loved ones and passed on messages for grieving folks left behind. Re-reading *We Don't Die* lifted my heart during those dreary first days following Michael's departure. I hung onto every word. I even dared to hope that some day *I* might receive a reading from Mr. Anderson.

After Michael left I began to read afterlife books with fervor. In addition to George Anderson, I read Sylvia Browne, James Van Praagh and later John Edward. Eventually, I became a regular viewer of Mr. Edward's *Crossing Over* TV program.

As far as religious beliefs, I didn't belong to any particular denomination. My mother was raised a Seventh Day Adventist and my dad came from a long line of Quakers, but he leaned toward agnosticism. I had attended Catholic Marymount University but had studied Eastern philosophy in my early twenties. I had meditated daily, sat in lotus position, chanted Hindu phrases, burned incense and had my own guru in an ashram located off Nebraska Avenue in Northwest, D.C. It seemed to bring me a sense of real peace. I recall being quite an idealist back in those days, reed thin with long brown, straight hair parted in the middle.

After college I began to peruse Norman Vincent Peale, becoming a Positive Thinker for a bit. I gained a sense of control over my life with Positive Thinking. What I liked best about Norman Vincent Peale was his down-to-earth way of looking at things. He preached, yes, but the manner in which he broadcast his message was always natural and practical. I could make my life better by simply trusting Jesus and putting my life in God's capable hands.

But after years of weathering misfortunes, including my mother's illness, Jo's bouts with severe psoriasis, a beloved longtime boyfriend leaving me to marry someone else he'd only known a few weeks, the murder of several friends, escalating anxiety attacks and various other hard knocks, my faith had dwindled down to a sputtering candle flame.

Then I met Michael.

From January until July we were joyful, almost ecstatically so. The pinnacle of our relationship seemed to occur on Independence Day 1997. We drove down to Old Town Manassas for the holiday. We first stopped at a couple of antique stores on the way, just to browse. The weather was in the mid-eighties, quite pleasant for July, and puffy white sheep clouds ambled across the sky. Meteorologists predicted a slight chance of thunderstorms but they never materialized.

Mike and I wandered all over the quaint Norman Rockwell town. Nothing seemed to be open, but we window-shopped and acted like silly kids, joking and swinging from the old caboose down by the tracks. He was wearing his garish red Hawaiian shirt, tan shorts and a baseball cap. He looked just like a big twelve-year-old. I wore my tie dyed skirt, teal silk blouse and fancy jeweled sandals. It was a wonder that I could traipse anywhere in that fussy footwear! I was L'Oreal blonde at that point in my life, with hair slightly below my shoulders. I snapped several pictures that day with my Olympus, and when I look at them now, my eyes moisten with tears. With the sunlit primary colors and late afternoon shadows we resembled figures in an Edward Hopper painting. We kept expecting a train to pass through town but we were disappointed.

On the drive back to Michael's house, we turned up the Oldies 100 station and sang boisterously to 50's and 60's tunes. If there is a heaven, then it must be like that evening as we cruised along Route 28, windows rolled down, deep purple and tangerine sundown as our backdrop. But by the time we ate our fried chicken dinners at the Fairfax City Roy Rogers restaurant near Mike's house, he seemed to be much subdued, suddenly tired. We had planned on viewing the fireworks at nearby Fairfax High School but I decided to go home after spending a few minutes at Mike's.

The next night Michael stopped by my house to watch the movie *Picnic,* starring William Holden and Kim Novak. When he first came in the door, Jo showed him the new dining room wallpaper, hung only two days earlier. She also brought his attention to her impressive, growing Barbie doll collection on display in our illuminated china cabinet. Michael had been teasing her for some time about "playing with Barbie dolls at her age" until he actually saw the exquisite fashion figures. His eyes glittered with emotional tears when he viewed the meticulously detailed Rhett Butler and Scarlett O'Hara dolls, attired in the finest silk, lace and velvet. "Oh Jo, they're so pretty! I had no idea." he exclaimed.

Then we all went into the den to watch *Picnic*. He enjoyed the classic story about a handsome drifter making a big impact on a small Kansas town during Labor Day festivities but he was especially quiet the entire evening; he was not making his usual droll comments on the film. I noticed he didn't even want the Mickey's ale I offered him. He sat very close to me on our burgundy loveseat, arm draped around my shoulders. Occasionally he'd draw me close and give me a gentle kiss. Michael was always an affectionate person, a trait I found most endearing. After the video I thought we might grab a midnight snack at the local Metro Diner since he had indicated that he wanted to do that earlier. However, when midnight came, he merely wanted to stroll around the block with me and he insisted he wasn't hungry. Somewhere in the back of my mind a very faint alarm bell began to ring. I could not put my finger on it, but something was just not right.

A week later, he called me from his shop around three o'clock. It was a miserable steambath of a Saturday afternoon as only Washington area summer days can be. Michael wanted to close down his business early and visit Green Spring Park, a block from the Salvation Army. On the way to work that morning he had stopped his car to rescue a bewildered box tortoise from the highway and had released the little fellow at Green Spring. He said he wanted to see if the reptile remained somewhere on the grounds. We got there and looked for the critter but ended up wading in the stream and petting the ducks and geese that lived in the park instead. We never found the tortoise. After wading in the blessedly refreshing water, Mike and I put our shoes back on, rolled down the legs of our faded jeans and sat on a wooden bench at the top of the hill.

The merciless sun filtered through the tall trees, nary a hint of a breeze stirring the leaves. Then Michael began to talk, prefacing his speech with a warm hug and a passionate kiss and the words, "Oh Rosy. I love you *so* much!" But as he said this, his eyes appeared to be glistening with tears. I felt bewildered as he continued, "I don't know what you would do if I ever had to leave you. Would you be all right? Honey, I can't be responsible for all your happiness. I know your life is so hard back home, with your mom and all. But I think there's something wrong with me,

Pee Wee, something really wrong. I don't feel like myself lately. I might not be around for much longer. I just don't know...Please pray for me, Rosy. I don't ever want to leave you!"

I was completely thunderstruck. Yet I embraced him and reassured him that I would pray for him. "You're never going to leave, Mike!" I cried. "We'll never lose each other!" In all honesty I could not console him that I would "be all right," however. He lay down on the bench, head in my lap. He said that his heart hurt at times and he planned to visit a doctor that coming Monday. I then offered to take him there but by now I was truly worried. I knew that Michael did not trust doctors and rarely visited them. The afternoon of July 12, 1997 was soul-searing hot, yet a chill shivered up and down my spine. I began to feel dizzy, sick, suffocated. Nothing he'd said made logical sense to me.

My dazed heart whispered,
"This is the beginning of the end."

Chapter Four

Shiny New Chapter

Ah, but our beginning! Looking back on it, I can see that Michael and I were destined to meet, fated to fall in love. Every lover believes this, of course, as they read their time-honored lines in the play of life. The drama is as old as mankind itself but to each of us the script is exhilarating and new as we perform our roles, hearts beating wildly in apparent affinity. Only the playwright knows how the melodrama will end.

Perhaps the most extraordinary thing about our first meeting was how many years transpired before it finally took place. Michael had owned and operated his bookstore and TV repair shop a mere four-and-a-half miles from my doorstep since the early 1970's. The same year that he established his business in Bailey's Crossroads, I had attended nearby Congressional School for the first time as a freshman. Although I didn't know it at the time, one of my good friends from that school was having her television sets serviced by Mike on a regular basis. Unknown to both of us, in those days Michael and I often shopped at the same stores, partied at the same nightclubs and ate at the same restaurants.

During the seventies, eighties and nineties I had occasion to drive past Mike's store innumerable times while running errands at the adjacent shopping centers. For years, I also created freelance calligraphy at Skyline Mall, located very close to Mike's Books. I might have glanced over at his small shop but I never stopped. Michael had a daily habit of visiting the

Alexandria Salvation Army on his way to work; our friend Ed was finding bargains at the same Salvation Army store every morning for several years at the same time. While doing so, Ed befriended a man who was also a regular Army customer. After I met Mike I discovered that both Mike and Ed had shared close mutual friendship with this gentleman for a long time!

The karmic tumblers in the safe were falling methodically into place as the years rolled by but you might say that it was wild British blues rocker Eric Burdon of "The Animals" fame who finally cracked the safe open that led to my meeting Michael. Sometime during the summer of 1987 Jo developed quite a crush on Eric after watching him sing "We Gotta Get out of This Place" in one of those frivolous beach movies that were so popular back in the early 60's. She bought all The Animals records she could find after that and soon they were occupying a lot of real estate in our basement. Her ardor for Mr. Burdon waned as time went on. By 1996 she decided to sell a number of the LP's at our June yard sale, but apparently nobody was an Animals fan that day, so after the sale ended, we hauled the lot back into our living room for temporary storage. A couple months went by and the records still sat in the room. Dad was growing irritated with us for not returning them to our basement or giving them away to the thrift store and he was nagging us about it on a daily basis. Finally I had heard enough and the next day, August 12, 1996 I searched the voluminous Northern Virginia Yellow Pages, seeking a music or record store that bought and sold recordings.

There were perhaps fifteen listings and I called each one of them. Nobody bought records anymore, only CDs. I was on the verge of giving up when I saw that only one name remained: Mike's Records. With a defeated sigh I dialed the number. After the first ring a mellow voice answered, "Mike's!" I instantly pictured a laid back Jerry Garcia sort of man, bear-like, bearded and independent, a "character" perhaps.

"Do you buy records?" I stammered.
"Yes."

"How about old British rock albums like The Animals?"

"Sure. Bring em by and I'll have a look at em."

I asked him his exact location in Bailey's Crossroads and he told me, quite succinctly. Then I asked him how late he stayed open.

"Until six," he intoned. And that was the end of our conversation. It certainly didn't sparkle like the witty dialogue in movie romances and I was completely unaware of what was shaping up for the next day.

Tuesday, August 13th was miserably, hideously hot and yet I grabbed my nearest top, a dark green sweatshirt with a big black cat face silk-screened on it. I no sooner had pulled it over my head than I regretted wearing the damn thing but Jo was eager to go. It was nearly one o'clock and we had not even eaten our lunch. After transporting the surplus Eric Burdon albums, a Mindbenders poster and assorted 1960's British rock fan magazines to the car, we drove to Mike's Records. From the outside the shop looked small and rather quirky: TV sets, antiques, books and records displayed in the front window. A little bell over the door jingled when we stepped into the welcome coolness. I felt as if I were walking into a Victorian chapter in a Dickens story. We intended to show the proprietor the goods, get a small bit of cash in exchange and leave in five minutes or so, anticipating an Arby's lunch.

Three hours later we were still there.

Mike was not like Jerry Garcia at all! He was a charming, incredibly engaging man looking years younger than his true age. I found him quite cute in a boy-like way and I noticed some other lady customers eyeing him that day. That sweltering afternoon, Jo, Mike and I discussed nearly our entire life histories. We felt so much at home that it was very difficult to believe we hadn't known one another forever. Because we talked about Iowa, I mentioned liking the MacKinlay Kantor novel *Spirit Lake*. "Oh,

I just bought that book this morning at the Salvation Army!" he proclaimed. Synchronicity was making inroads already. He spoke of growing up in small town Sigourney, Iowa, a short distance from where my Dad had spent his boyhood in Iowa City. Some of my father's relatives had even called Sigourney home for awhile.

I admired Mike's collage, an enormous piece of artwork that occupied most of a wall. I could see how much effort and emotion went into the creation of it and it worked very nicely on an artistic level as well. I had never seen anything like it. He had layered various photos clipped from *National Geographic*, *Smithsonian*, *Condé Nast Travel*, *Reader's Digest*, *The New Yorker* and other magazines into a wonderfully woven visual array. There were lots of sunset images, storms, wildlife, some interesting portraits and several witty cartoons included. "This is really amazing!" I exclaimed. "So many of these photos that you've pasted on the collage I've admired myself over the years. This collage is *you*, tells me so much about you!"

Mike just beamed. "Thanks," he said shyly. But eventually I glanced at my watch and was aghast to see that it was four o'clock. He went to his cash drawer and handed Jo twenty-five dollars for her items and then it was time to go. He said, "Sometimes I need somebody to do lettering, you know, make signs for my shop. Would you be interested?" I handed him my calligraphy business card. He smiled at both of us but patted Jo on the shoulder and said, "Goodbye ladies. It was really swell talking to you. Like old home week, wasn't it?" Ridiculous as it sounds, I felt a tiny twinge of jealousy at the patting gesture. Then we opened the door and drove away into the blast furnace heat.

In the ensuing months I often thought of Michael but I doubted that he was doing the same with me. He never called my business card number. He told me much later that he'd wanted to call but thought it might be too bold, too presumptuous. I had a vague idea that at some point I would sell him one of my historical documents since he bought ephemera as well as records. This brittle, sepia-toned paper was a 1791 slave contract that had been salvaged from an old drugstore which had burned to the ground in my Mom's hometown of Pamplin, Virginia back in the 1920's. I didn't like being its owner since I believed slavery was a terrible sin. The thought of someone suffering all those years ago made me uneasy and sad. But it *was* an excuse to return to his shop. Then another notion entered my head.

During our amazing August 13th marathon conversation, Mike had talked about his love of music. He had handed us a card stating that he was "The World's Oldest Living Teenager" and performed at parties, singing oldies accompanied by his guitar. Serendipitously at the time, I was creating music on my computer, composing songs and orchestrating them with digital instruments. There is an acronym for this: MIDI, meaning Musical Instrument Digital Interface. You input notes into a special software program called a sequencer or you can play directly from your MIDI keyboard or other instrument. The end result can be as lavishly arranged or as simple as you like. MIDI files are very small but one drawback was that the format could not reproduce the human voice singing words; it was completely instrumental.

Years earlier I had composed a tearjerker country rock song that I had penned lyrics for and titled "My Crazy Heart." Someday I wanted to have a man perform the song and play guitar while I recorded it. I hoped to interest someone in Nashville in the music (yeah, right!) Maybe Michael was just the man for the job! It would do no harm to pay another visit to his shop and ask, would it? I created a tape of the song and printed out the lyrics from my computer.

It was two days before Christmas when Jo and I finally got around to seeing Mike again. Since the last time we had seen him, we had discovered to our utter surprise that we had a half brother from Mom's previous marriage. The uncanny thing is we got a call from our unknown brother Bruce the same August 13th day that we had met Michael. With the holidays approaching, we decided to throw a bash for the newfound family, scheduling it for Saturday, December 28th. We invited our half sister Barbara, some neighbors and a few friends. It was Jo's idea to hire Michael to entertain at the party.

The little bell tinkled over the door of the shop and Michael glanced up as he saw us enter. He was wearing an enormous faux fur Russian hat and had "half glasses" perched on his nose, the kind of magnifying readers that you buy at a drugstore. He recognized us right away and said "Hi girls!" I felt my heart skip a beat. We got down to business about hiring him for the party and I handed him the tape of my song, along with the lyric sheet. He glanced at them and carefully set them down atop somebody's TV that he was repairing. We decided to partially trade in the historical document I had brought in exchange for his normal fee of $75.00 to perform at our upcoming Christmas fête.

Even though Mike was friendly enough, I couldn't help but feel somewhat disappointed. He seemed to be in a hurry, eager to get to the bank to deposit his earnings before they closed at 2:00 p.m. Also his mother Miriam was visiting him that day. It was the first time I had met her and I felt kinship with her but she soon began to talk to Jo, mostly about her cats, Stripes and TomTom. (Little did I know at that time but Jo and I would one day own those very same kitties.) Since Jo was occupied with Miriam in the back room, Mike and I were left alone in the main room.

He was standing in front of the collage and his hat and glasses were off by then and he really looked quite handsome, his dark brown hair just long enough to be soft and feathery as it spilled over his collar. His face was a nearly perfect oval. A quick glance showed me that he was wearing tight, faded jeans, a black leather vest with a brass sheriff badge pinned to it and a long-sleeved, nondescript flannel shirt. His swarthy good looks hinted at his Native American and Spanish ancestry, although I knew from our previous conversation that he also came from Scottish and Swiss stock.

I was facing him, my back against his TV workbench.

"I still can't get over how impressive your collage is, Mike!" I said, meaning every word.

"You really *do* like it, don't you?" he said, suddenly beaming and lighting up the room. When he smiled, the grin had a rather bashful quality because he didn't show his teeth. I grin the same way; I am told it is an "introverted" smile. "Nobody else seems to even notice it." He grew quite animated, chatting about some of the photos on the wall and he began to really look at me, to give me a searching, deep gaze. We were the same height and our eyes locked in a sudden flash of recognition, a deep bond that I was surprised to find happening to us. It really felt like an electrical current passed between the two of us, conveyed solely by our eyes and our proximity to each other. It was as if we were both thinking, "Oh. It's *you*, at long last. It's been so many years, so many lifetimes! I've missed you terribly." It was literally a magnetic moment and I knew he felt it too. I saw it in his soft brown, intelligent eyes. I felt a bit flustered and I'm certain I was blushing as my cheeks grew warm.

All too soon it was time to go. Miriam and Jo came from the back room and we said our good-byes. "Remember, eight o'clock Saturday!" Jo said.

"Oh. I need your phone number!" Mike replied. "I'll call before I come," he said. "And I'll need directions getting there." Since I was always the "direction" person in the family, I drew a quick map for him to follow.

"Miriam, you're welcome to come to the party," Jo and I chimed. Michael glanced over at us a bit sharply.

"Well, thank you so much, but I don't drive after dark. Thanks for asking though. You all have a good time now," she said.

Michael looked visibly relieved. I found out later that he didn't particularly want his mother to attend the party as he thought her presence might make him more nervous. I also found out from Marion at a later date that poor Michael had developed a major case of pre-performance butterflies in his stomach after he agreed to accept the engagement. Unknown to us, "The World's Oldest Living Teenager" had only played a handful of gigs in his life! But the peculiar thing is, he had begun to practice a repertoire of oldies music just two weeks before we hired him. He felt compelled to rehearse every night, as if he were anticipating an upcoming event.

I felt rather confused by what had happened or rather what *didn't* happen that afternoon. I sensed Mike was attracted to me as I was to him but then I convinced myself that he was simply a cool, musician guy that we had hired to entertain our guests. Even though he was down-home Iowa friendly to people, paradoxically he also projected an attitude of detachment and macho coolness with his demeanor. It was an unusual combination and I found myself intrigued by the man.

Chapter Five

And We Danced

The party was coming up quickly and there was little time to dwell on this Mike person while a mind-boggling amount of work needed to be done in preparation for our guests on Saturday. Jo and I toiled away, cleaning our three story house, baking cookies, buying snack platters and refreshments, putting up holiday decorations and getting Mom spiffed up. Finally everything was starting to look really beautiful. We had a near disaster the day before the party when Dad brought home an ugly, rusty old hospital bed from the local thrift store and parked it prominently in the middle of our newly polished living room floor! It looked *dreadful* and we were furious at him, since we had told him repeatedly not to buy it until *after* the party. It scraped up the walls and floor and Jo was livid with rage, as was I; we nearly came to blows over the contraption. That's how keyed up we were. We considered canceling the party entirely, but we decided to haul the ancient bed outside, out of sight in the back yard. And Saturday arrived.

The chilly and sunny day was busy and Mike called about seven and briefly talked to Jo, verifying his appointment later that night. A sudden disturbing thought popped into my head. Suppose this Mike couldn't sing or play guitar at all? What if he had a "tin ear" and we were all in for an evening of off-key hound dog hollering accompanied by sour guitar "chords"? I groaned inwardly. After all we *were* hiring him without ever having heard a single note of music emanating from him! The thought only added to my uneasiness.

I dressed up in my old-fashioned purple velvet skirt, lacy

white blouse and black velvet vest. Bruce and Barbara and their families arrived and we took photos with Mom, upstairs in her room. I was getting increasingly nervous as 8:00 loomed. I chattered and bustled about like a jittery sparrow. Then the doorbell rang and Jo trotted downstairs to answer it. I heard her say in her best flirtatious voice, "Oh *hi*, Mike!"

As I heard Jo's lilting tones, I guessed she had a few ideas of her own concerning the (hopefully) talented Mr. Hardesty. I was still in Mom's room, snapping photos of the family but I thought, "Enough of this. Time to glide gracefully down the stairs in my holiday finery!" I peered into Mom's ornate French Provincial dresser mirror one more time, making sure everything was in place. An uncertain yet eager lady looked back at me. I guess I looked pretty foxy. I sure hoped so.

I cleared my throat and headed down the stairway. As I descended, the most amazing thing happened. In the movie *Gone With the Wind* there is a scene at Twelve Oaks where Scarlett is ascending the steps and she peers down to see Rhett Butler looking up at her with that piercing, heart-fluttering glance. It's one of my favorite parts of the movie. Not to be a cliché, but the same thing happened to me! Yes, I was Scarlett floating gracefully downstairs, slender hand on the banister and Michael/Rhett was standing down below, debonair under the crystal chandelier looking up at me with that *look*. We smiled at each other, a quiet, deep, knowing smile with our eyes. I could feel a connection with him that was like an ancient lock and key fitting together. I knew we had done this same thing in another lifetime or two or...

My heartbeat quickened and I said, "Don't you look nice tonight!"

He replied, "Thank you. You look very nice too!" And he couldn't help his eyes traveling appreciatively from the top of my head, down my body, to the tips of my boots peeking out demurely from my purple skirt. I blushed. (I tend to do that. Hence the nickname Rosy I guess). I noted that he was attired like Elvis, black leather jacket, red satin shirt, tight straight-legged jeans and black penny loafers. His dark shiny hair was carefully combed back from his forehead to complete the Nifty Fifties look. Now, if only he could sing and play as good as he looked, all would be perfect.

I wasn't sure where Jo had disappeared to but I was glad she wasn't around. I asked Mike if he was all set up with his guitar, microphone and other equipment and he said, "Oh sure. Your sister showed me where I could put my stuff in the basement."

I thought to myself, "Ha! I bet she showed you!" We walked from the hallway to the den. It felt so natural walking beside him like that. I asked if I could get him a Budweiser. He said thanks, yes. I went to the kitchen to get him the beer and one for myself. When I returned to the den I saw to my dismay that Dad had cornered Mike and apparently was reminiscing about his boyhood times in Iowa. Dad had a book opened and was showing Michael photos of the various Iowa counties. I knew that their conversation would go on for quite some time, as they both had some common ground to cover, so I just handed Mike his beer and he smiled and took it from me. For a man, he had such a sweet, boyish smile. I left to attend to my other guests, but was secretly wishing we had not invited anyone else.

Most of the rest of the evening was a blur of bustling about, serving drinks, eggnog, platter goodies, Christmas cookies, showing folks where the powder room was, laughing, and just being a hostess. One rather inebriated guest bumped up against lit red candles in the dining room while trying to grab chicken wings from the platter, spilling crimson wax on our French wallpaper and draperies.

I had lost track of Mike and didn't hear him playing or singing yet. At 10:00 sharp as I was standing in the dining room, discussing dollhouse draperies with a pleasant but loquacious lady, I heard the first chords of "House of the Rising Sun" blasting out. Ah, the concert had begun. After some polite minutes I made my way down to the basement. Nearly all the guests were already there. At that point Mike was playing Chubby Checker's "Let's Twist Again (Like We Did Last Summer)." I sidled up to the metal folding chairs that we had arranged around his "stage." I took note that Barbara and Jo were sitting center stage. Barbara's other brother Richard was videotaping the party.

Almost as soon as I arrived, Michael began to look at me, smiling again with that devil boy grin. I loved the way his hands moved nimbly over the guitar's fingerboard and strummed, so capable and somehow strong. He knew what he was doing and it sounded wonderful. He played, he joked, he sang, he told stories about his days in the Navy. He had a whole nightclub patter going. Maybe I imagined it, but he seemed charged with electricity, so animated. I was slightly giddy myself, with a couple of Buds and Bartles & Jaymes wine coolers under my satin belt. He started teasing me about the two of us forming a rock group called "Rosy and The Originals" but then he laughed, "I think that name's already been taken. But I do like your voice, Rosy. You sing so sweetly!" I know my face turned crimson when he said that but I felt very happy at the same time.

When he took his break, he brushed past me, and handed me his beautiful, white electric guitar. "Would you mind looking after this until I come back?" he said quietly, "I trust you with it." I took it gently and handled it like a baby. I knew how precious it was to him. I plunked the strings playfully and was mortified to hear a very loud TWANG come from the amps! Luckily he was out of the room at the time.

Finally around midnight the guests began to leave and Mike packed up his equipment. The concert was over. I felt disappointed as I assumed he would leave along with the other guests. But after sending my older brother and sister into the cold, star-studded December night, I noted that Mike was still in the house, standing at the front door next to Dad. They really seemed to hit it off that night. I was very glad to have bonded with my siblings and was pleased that the party was quite a success.

Jo, ever resourceful, asked Michael, "I know! Before you go, would you like to see some of our 3D artwork on our computers? We even have an interactive 'Titanic' game that we've started playing!"

"That sounds really interesting," he said as he willingly followed us down to the basement recreation room once again.

We spent the next two hours looking at old family albums, computer art and talking. Mike was incredibly impressed with Jo's enormous and unbelievably detailed Southern mansion dollhouse, with its fancy chandeliers, inlaid wood floors and a tiny music room with grand piano, trumpet and violin! He chuckled over a wee stalk of broccoli "cooking" in a minute copper saucepan sitting on a cast-iron kitchen stove.

When Mike saw the very realistic "Titanic" computer game he told us some amusing tales about the Navy, including one about being seasick into his hat when he was ordered to salute an officer! I sensed that although he liked Jo, he was sitting closer to me, looking into my eyes more and touching me occasionally with his hand on my arm, when he wanted to make a strong point about some idea we were discussing.

When I showed him my pen and ink stipple drawing of a local train station, "Point Of Rocks" he got very quiet and thoughtful and a strange look came over his face. "You know, with your permission, I'd love to make prints of these and try to sell them as signed and numbered limited editions at my bookstore," he said. "I know the guy next door who runs the print shop and I performed for his wedding, so he owes me one. And he does a really great job. He's very conscientious about his work. In fact, I'd like to print these two, also." He indicated a drawing of my Francis Scott Key House and a portrait of two little girls I had created. I was flattered and told him that we would arrange it. It finally was time for him to go as it had been a long day for all of us and he had a ten-mile drive ahead of him to his home in Fairfax.

We three went outside, helping him put his equipment into his station wagon. Mike may have been small and wiry, yet he was quite strong physically. It felt good being beside him, helping him pack up. As he put the last amp in the car, he turned to Jo and me, "Thanks for a wonderful evening, ladies." We told him we thoroughly enjoyed the party and we praised his musical abilities; and we meant it. We joked about his KC Jones license plate, talked about trains and Arlo Guthrie's "City of New Orleans" for a bit until it got a little awkward with Mike standing there, looking suddenly shy, glancing down at his loafers. He looked like a bashful teenager to me and my heart went out to him. I could tell he did not want to go home. I sensed that he was a very lonely soul.

Purely on impulse, I ran into the house and grabbed a $20 bill from Mom's purse hanging in the hall closet — shame on me! I handed the money to Mike, "Here, this is for you. For playing such a fine concert." He refused it, at first. I saw Jo looking daggers at me. She knew me too well! She knew what I was up to and she also guessed that the money was not mine but was Mom's. She probably wondered why *she* hadn't come up with the plan first. He finally took it and thanked me, tears brimming his eyes. I was not accustomed to seeing a man cry. He impetuously grabbed me and hugged me very tightly. I could smell the rich leather of his jacket, his after-shave. He turned his head and I must have turned mine too because I could feel his cheek against my cheek. It felt surprisingly smooth and warm, just a hint of masculine stubble. Time had no meaning at that point. He kissed me on my right cheek. Then he withdrew from me and quickly hugged and kissed Jo.

He turned to open his car door but instead rushed back to hug and kiss me again on the cheek, only this time harder. He spoke, his voice cracking slightly, "Thank you so much. You don't know how enjoyable this evening has been for me," he whispered. And I guess because he was feeling so emotional, he knew that he must go. He backed the car out of the driveway, waved at us with a sad little grin and was gone.

Chapter Six

Cherish the Moment

Two days later the phone rang and Jo answered it. "This is the grandpa who showed up at your party the other night!" Mike quipped. "When I finally got home and took a look at myself in the mirror, oh my God, I looked like road-kill. I'm surprised you girls didn't kick me out! Any reviews come in about my performance?" Jo laughed loudly and told him that he was quite a hit. Then he asked if I was nearby. Slightly annoyed, she handed the phone to me. "Hi Rosy, how are you doing? Ready to make that record with me?" he said, "I have my guitar, mic and amp set up here at the bookstore. We can make a tape of funny voices! We can imitate people and have all kinds of fun. While you're at it, bring the artwork in and we'll have it printed. Make sure you bring those big photo albums with you too. I want to look at them again."

When he spoke the next sentence my heart caught in my throat. "I'd love to take you to lunch sometime soon."

"Oh you don't have to do that Mike!" I stuttered.

"It's not that I have to but I really *want* to!" he answered.

"Well, maybe," I demurred.

I was slightly taken aback but I was also swept up in his enthusiasm so Jo and I drove to Bailey's Crossroads, requisite items in tow. As opposed to the other two times we had visited, on this occasion I felt quite nervous. When we got there we found the shop full of people, including several guys who turned out to be Mike's old friends. Miriam was there too but she didn't stay long. She smiled at Jo and me and said, "This is my favorite place in the whole *world* to visit. Mike's Books is always interesting. Everyone eventually comes here!" She waved farewell and was out the door into the nippy, bright afternoon.

After some chitchat Michael took us next door to meet his good friend Bob the printer. Bob was a wonderfully pleasant Vietnamese fellow and he agreed to print the three pieces of stipple artwork on rich, slightly textured, acid-free paper. They would look very classy printed that way, he assured us. I handed the drawings over to him, a bit apprehensively nonetheless. I knew how many hundreds of hours had gone into the creation of those babies, applying single dots of ink with a technical pen to form a grayscale image. Stipple technique is not for the impatient.

Bob photographed the originals while we waited and then he returned them to me. I felt relieved to have them back in hand. We thanked Bob and headed back to Mike's shop for awhile.

He was teasing and friendly to us, me especially. When he laughed the world lit up and it contrasted with his regular expression which was quite serious and studious. He was poring over our photo albums again, especially the photos taken of Jo and me as wee tykes during our summer holiday at Lake Okoboji, Iowa. "Awwwww. Look at little Rosy!" he exclaimed. He affectionately patted the black and white snapshots with his fingers. "You kids have pixie haircuts I see," he observed. We certainly did. The barber had nearly scalped us the week before the trip and we were miserable with our bobbed hair. But apparently Mike found the hairdos charming so I smiled at him. He smiled back at me and wrapped his arm around my waist, hugging me briefly. We left a short while later and he promised us he would call soon about the prints.

Two days later an early January storm blew in, bringing snow, ice and howling winds. Around two in the afternoon, the phone rang and I picked it up.

"Jo? Is that you Jo?" Mike's voice came over the wires.

"No, it's Rosy," I said, "Want me to go get my sister?"

There was a slight pause on the line and I suddenly felt

doubtful and unhappy. He had called to talk to Jo! What was going on? I was sure he had been drawn to me but...

"No, that's OK. I just thought your voice sounded like Jo's. So how are you Rosy? I didn't go to work today because of the weather. Only the second time in twenty-six years I've taken off. I love snow and am happy as a clam out here in my house with my cats and books! This is a vacation for me." I laughed and our conversation flowed for over three hours. Once again, we discussed ideas from A to Z: our recent Christmas party, Voltaire, art, music, philosophy, Iowa, snow, cats, thunderstorms, Virginia, his former career with the telephone company, fears, dreams...it went on and on but it never grew tiresome. To the contrary; I felt extremely energized!

He expressed interest in the lyrics of the "Crazy Heart" song and wondered whom I cared about when I had penned it. I explained that it was created when I was with my former boyfriend Paul. He'd decided to abandon me after years together and marry a girl he'd just met weeks before. "Maybe someday you'll write a song like that about me," he said. "Only I won't leave you." I knew then that the bond I felt was mutual. It was all very natural, the way it was meant to be. That was when I realized his voice sounded so much like famed actor William Hurt's; soothing and melodious with a hint of Midwest twang. He had a nice laugh too and a wicked little snicker.

He ended our long conversation by saying, "I sure wish you were over here with me. I wish I could pull you right over the phone line, Rosy. I feel so comfortable with you. How come you're such an interesting person?" Then he said in a near-whisper, "I think I'll nickname you 'Heart'."

I was thrilled to hear those words.

I replied, "I feel the same way. I'm glad you called today. You really brightened my afternoon!" When I prepared dinner that night I felt euphoric. I suspected I was falling fast but I didn't care.

Michael came over the very next Saturday after telling Jo cryptically on the phone that he wanted to stop by. He said he was scheduled to fix our next door neighbors' TV set, having given them his number at our party the previous week. I peeked out the window but couldn't see any sign of his car. I kept looking at the clock, twiddling my thumbs nervously. Finally around 7:30 the doorbell rang and in stepped Mike, wearing his leather jacket and a stylish black felt cowboy hat rimmed ornamentally with silvery conchos. He looked wonderful and he toted some packages with him. As I brought him a beer, he told us that he had fixed our neighbors' set easily.

We all descended down to our basement and reclined on the couch, Michael in the middle. He showed us one of the objects that he brought with him, a richly illustrated book about lighthouses. He turned the pages as Jo and I looked at the volume and I thought, "One more thing we have in common, a love of lighthouses!" He put the publication on our "coffee table" which was really a large wicker sea chest. Then he produced a couple photo albums of his family. It was fascinating to see his two kids, his childhood sweetheart who later became his wife, his six grandkids and Michael himself when he was a young man. "Here's when I was a skinny, scrawny kid of fourteen and here I am six months later after eating Bob Hoffman's Weight Gain tablets and lifting weights," Mike said proudly.

"I used to eat those things too!" I laughed. And he did look remarkably different for such a short amount of time. With his serious expression and macho silent man poses in some photos, he reminded me of an adolescent Gary Cooper. I told him so.

"Yep," he agreed, "Tell you what, I'll leave these with you guys for a few days so you can look at them better." When we were looking at the pictures I was astonished to suddenly feel Mike's hand on my left knee, very gently caressing it. I suppose I should have been offended at the familiarity of the gesture but somehow it didn't seem forward at all but spontaneous. Then he took my left hand and held it for a few seconds, acting as if he was measuring my fingers. "You have really pretty hands, Rosy. They're so small and delicate and artistic. I love your hands." I thanked him and enjoyed the sensation of him holding my hand in his.

After looking at the books, Mike arose from the sofa and with a mischievous grin and twinkle in his eyes opened up the other package he had brought with him. I was amazed; it contained the prints, looking exquisite on the acid-free paper! Bob had done an excellent job and he had varied the colors of the background paper for more interest; some pictures had been lithographed on pure white, others on a creamy ivory. "Will you look at that? Those prints look absolutely *wonderful*, so professional, Mike! Wow, I can't get over it. Thanks so much for bringing them tonight," I exclaimed. "How many *did* you get printed?" I said, as he placed the hefty package of reproductions in my hands.

"Oh, a hundred of each. There should be three hundred there total." he said, "Please just sign them in pencil and number them when you get a chance and we'll put them up for sale at my store. Jo, maybe you can help us pick out some attractive mats for them?"

"Oh Wow they look great!" Jo concurred, "I know a place where we can get acid-free mats for a really good price and it's mail order." In the past Jo did my framing for me when I created pet portraits.

"Mike we'll go 50/50 on this, OK?" I said.

He looked happy and said, "Sure!" with a wave of his hand.

The three of us headed over toward the electronic keyboards. Jo played some tunes from our voluminous music fakebook on the Yamaha. She owned a Casio too and I usually played that instrument when we jammed. Then Mike spoke, "Hey Rosy, how about playing 'My Crazy Heart' for me so I can see how it's supposed to go? I'm not quite sure how the lyrics fit in with the music. What you put on the tape was instrumental." I turned on the Casio and played a G major chord, which is how the song began. I punched in the Country rhythm and began to sing the words tentatively, feeling rather silly. He smiled shyly and sidled over to me, standing close to me on my right. Then I began to perform a piece that I had composed when I was a kid. I was ten years old at the time and our class was learning the poem, "El Dorado." It had inspired me and I had created a simple song based on imagery in the poetry. I handed him a sheet of lyrics for it.

"This song is pretty lame, actually," I said, "I wrote it in the fifth grade after all!"

"What! You're kidding. Hey, I *am* impressed," he answered, "How is it that there was such wisdom in one so young? Huh?" He was smiling and his gaze appeared to be looking directly into my soul. Jo seemed to have disappeared; I think she mentioned something about getting dinner started. Michael and I were alone.

"We sure had a blast from the past at our party last week, didn't we?" I said.

"Yes, we did," he said, "But sometimes a party of two is the best party of all, don't you agree?" He took a step in my direction and began to hug me very tightly with his strong arms and I embraced him back, the most natural reaction in the world. Then he took my face in his hand and kissed me, this time firmly and directly on my lips. We held onto each other for a long time, just enjoying the propinquity, locked together in the basement, spotlighted by an overhead pool lamp on a dark January night.

Jo told me later that she had come back downstairs and she had seen us kissing through the woven screen of our folding wooden room divider. She was taken aback and a little vexed. But she thought we looked marvelous together. She said Mike's eyes were closed and he looked positively blissful. Mike cleared his throat and pulled away from me a little when he saw Jo. "Dinner is almost ready Rosy," Jo announced.

"Uh, dinner?" I repeated, starry-eyed, "Mike would you like to stay around for a bite to eat?"

He shook his head. "No, I appreciate the offer but I promised my daughter Monica I would call her around nine and here it is nine-thirty! Besides, Squeeky and Magic need their supper. Haven't fed them since before work this morning." Jo went upstairs then and I began to follow her but Michael looked intently at me and pulled me close again and kissed me a second time. We went up the carpeted steps and stood in the hallway. He reached for my hands and clasped them in his and then brushed them against his lips very tenderly. "Such sweet, pretty hands! And you create such wonderful things with them, honey," he murmured again, "Good-bye Rosy. Tell Jo I said thanks for everything. I had a swell time!" I opened the front door to the bitter cold and bid him farewell, smiling joyfully.

After that night we began to see each other regularly. I'd visit his shop once a week, usually on Wednesdays, and we talked on the phone several times a day. I'd call him in the afternoon and he always phoned me at six o'clock, closing time. Then he would get in touch with me nightly and we'd converse until well after midnight on some evenings. It was heady and I never felt so alive. He had even created several nicknames for me: "Pee Wee," "Pudder," "Heart" and "Posy." I called him "Mikey."

Michael stopped by my house on Valentine's Day, bearing flowers and candy. He meant to bring two Valentine cards for me too but in his nervousness he left them at the shop. Ed was over that night too and all four of us sang for hours. When Jo played "I Only Wanna Be with You," Mike looked directly at me and said, "I heard that on the radio just this afternoon! Listen to the words. That's exactly how I feel about you, Rosy." I knew the lyrics included the line, "I don't know what it is that makes me love you so, I only know I never wanna let you go." Later it says, "I never knew that I could be in love like this!" I basked in the glow of that moment. A week earlier Mike and I had eaten a late lunch at the local Chili's restaurant and he had made a tape for me that night, filled with his favorite songs, all of them impossibly mushy but oh how I loved that tape! I've played it so many times over the years that it's all worn out.

A few days later he produced the Cupid's Day cards. There it was, in his own handwriting, stated in black and white: *I love you*. At that point I felt confident enough to say back to him, "I love you too."

He made my birthday on February 28th a wonderful, sentimental occasion. He gifted me with a beautiful amethyst and silver ring, a silver jewelry chest engraved with "Rosy" in elegant Copperplate calligraphy and red silk roses among other thoughtful presents. I was sporting a new brown leather jacket and I smelled sweetly pretty with perfume he had bought. My brother Bruce, niece Sara, sister-in-law Paula and Ed were guests that night as well. We all drank some champagne and had a warm, happy time.

However, amid the festivities, I suddenly noticed Michael was missing from the dining room table. Nobody knew where he had gone but I found him sitting in the dark, on the living room couch. "Michael! What are you doing in here? Why did you leave the party?"

He looked sad and rather sheepish. "Oh I just was admiring this beautiful room. The decor is so old-fashioned and nice," he said, patting the cushion beside him. Michael was someone who always appreciated art and antiques. We had both in our house, especially vintage clocks.

"I can't thank you enough for all the thoughtful gifts and for being here tonight, babe," I whispered to him, hugging him so tightly. I wanted to reassure him that he had made my birthday the best one I had ever known. He seemed consoled yet his sudden shift in mood that February night worried me. He had looked quite depressed when I had come upon him unaware in the living room. But he departed an hour or so later in good spirits so I put my mind to rest.

Chapter Seven

A Place in the Sun

A week later, I visited his house off Guinea Road in Fairfax for the first time. It was a modest split-level in the charming Rutherford subdivision and I felt somewhat shy at first. For some reason, I had a sense of being ill at ease as I entered his home. Up until then, whenever Michael and I were together I always experienced a sense of peace and completeness. He often joked that he thought we were like the same person, the male and female halves of the same entity. Precisely how I would have described our relationship too.

"Come in my dear and see my etchings!" he joked as I stepped over the threshold. He handed me a glass of champagne, which I sipped delicately. He had Stevie Ray Vaughan playing loudly on his stereo and had red light bulbs glowing in his living room lamp and kitchen light fixtures.

I giggled, "A blast from my past, Mike! I used to have red light bulbs just like these! I think I bought them from Dart Drug or somewhere. They were supposed to be party lights that we switched on whenever we had a keg for the Glover Park posse," I said, referencing some of my past gatherings with friends from that part of Washington, D.C. "Only we put ours in the lamps that hung over our Minnesota Fats pool table." He laughed loudly. I halfway expected to see black light posters in fluorescent Day-Glo colors under ultraviolet rays. I thought I smelled incense, but actually he had lit several scented candles, concocting a mellow glow. He looked young and handsome in the tiny firelight. I relaxed a bit and he began to show me his extensive antiquarian book collection, proudly and gently opening the venerable volumes in their gilt bindings. Many books were first editions and a few dated back to the 1600's. Such a collection! He owned many steel engravings and other works of art, which I could appreciate.

Midway through the house tour, his little tabby Squeeky introduced herself to me. "Aw! Mike she is so adorable!" I exclaimed, picking kitty up in my arms and cuddling her tightly. Soon Magic made her debut too. She was soft and pretty as a bunny, and yet she had a curiously raspy short "meow." Mike grabbed her and deftly turned her upside down so I could see her tail-less rump. She probably thought this was most undignified but when he set her back down on the kitchen floor she rubbed her face up against his leg until he poured a saucer of milk for both little ladies.

The music, the lights and candles, the champagne, the proximity to the man I loved created their magic, as I knew they would. I took great care to mentally photograph that blustery March night and place it tenderly in my heart's album, to be cherished always. We made love for the first time that midnight and it was beyond words on every level. So this is what it felt like to be truly in love and to be loved in return!

It was with great reluctance that I left Mike's home that evening and I know that he was disappointed that I could not stay the night.

The calendar pages turned quickly and Spring came early that year after a mild winter. Michael and I took full advantage of the God-given warmth and were outdoors much of our time together, strolling through parks and getting to know each other better. At the end of March he helped me pick out a car, a 1988 Honda Accord. On Easter Sunday we purchased the automobile at the Westpark Hotel in Tyson's Corner and we proudly drove the sturdy little car back to my house. The previous owner had told me that he regularly traveled to the Adirondacks in the snow, driving the Accord! I could tell that he parted with the car reluctantly and he had maintained it diligently.

Not unexpectedly, Dad had an earful of unprintable things to say about the dark charcoal gray sedan but I was very proud of my "new" wheels and of my boyfriend. Mike was such a helpful person, always willing to lend a hand to make someone else's life a little easier; so much of his time and money was spent on others. *He was a steady, beautiful light in this dark, selfish world.* He also accompanied me to the DMV to get the title and registration settled. Then he handed me an envelope. "Here you are, Pee Wee. You are now the official owner of a Honda!" he grinned. The card showed a photo of some well-muscled hunks on the front and asked, "How many guys do you count?" Inside the punch line was "Depends. Are you a curvy blonde with a new sports car and loose morals?" And Mike had added, "You are *now*!" I laughed and replied, "Oh hell! You look a million times better than any of those guys, Mikey! I don't want them. I want *you!*" He chuckled and hugged me.

For our first official drive in the Honda, he made a special "Rosy's New Car" cassette, chock full of vintage tunes culled from his vast record collection. We took a drive out near his house that April night, Michael at the wheel. It was rather foggy and damp and he drove for a long time past George Mason University and down Ox Road. I began to get uneasy. I could feel anxiety starting to rise inside. I had no idea where we were going but we were heading south toward Lorton and Woodbridge. He wanted to show me his daughter's former house near a small pond in a housing development at Fairfax Station.

"Mike, I hate to say this but I'm getting a goddam panic attack!" I warned him, cracking open the window. "Could we please turn around and go back home?" The night sky was pitch black and the mist was very eerie, rising off the roadway.

"Oh poor Pudder," he said glancing over at me in concern. "We're almost there. Just a mile or so. Will you be all right?"

I swallowed, breathed deeply, squeezed my eyes shut and said, "Yes" weakly, but my heart was racing and I was feeling nauseous and a bit dizzy. My stomach was beginning to cramp.

Breathing was hard because I tended to take shallow breaths when I got these dreadful episodes. Every time I got an anxiety attack, I felt so angry with myself for being so vulnerable, so "weak" and yet the symptoms always came on strongly, involuntarily and I had very little control over them. I had been upfront with Mike right from the beginning of our relationship about the disorder, so he wasn't surprised by my nervousness that night. We looked at the house and turned back toward Fairfax. Inwardly, I breathed a big sigh of relief but the anxiety still rose in waves until we were back at his house. Like most anxiety sufferers, I was often less prone to attacks when I was in the driver's seat, when I was in charge. I think it's a question of feeling in control or not.

I felt embarrassed, like such a "wimpadoodle" for showing nervousness in front of Michael but he had a completely understanding attitude. "It's okay, Rose. I know how hard these things must be for you," he said patting my shoulder. "I'm reading the workbook I bought the other day, the one about panic disorder and I'm trying to figure it all out." He always had a keen interest in psychology. I took his free hand and squeezed it. "I love you Mike. For being there, for understanding, for *everything*."

He clasped my hand back, smiling softly. "I love you too, Rosy," he whispered.

Reminiscing, I can see that April was a wonderful, happy month for us. It was simply cherry blossoms and moonlight. It was feeling alive, wild and free. It was as perfect as the poets write it, but it was never "the cruelest month."

May arrived and Mike came over to my house to celebrate Mom's birthday on May Day. Several neighbors were also invited to the dinner party that evening. I remember all of us going outside to look at the Hale-Bopp comet after our meal. Michael was at his most charming, bearing gifts for Mom, who unfortunately could not make it downstairs. But she listened to him serenade her with his guitar in her room. I remember he played The

Brothers Four "Green Fields" and "Unchained Melody" by The Righteous Brothers and a Malaguena Spanish tune. Mom smiled sweetly and clapped her hands in appreciation. This wasn't the first time he had been kind to my mother. He had given her numerous little surprise gifts over the previous months and I appreciated it more than he could ever know. He was the same way toward Jo, showering her with unexpected presents. Each time he shopped at the Salvation Army, he would keep his eye and wallet open for thoughtful keepsakes he could give to his friends and family.

The next weekend was Mother's Day and we spent a Hallmark greeting card Sunday at his house, taking pictures of each other in the park and golden May sunlight. There are several creeks in Rutherfod Park and Mike liked to pose near them, one time going so far as to scamper over the rocks and stand directly in the middle of the flowing water, hands on hips, mugging for the camera. In the next picture, he is perched rather precariously on the iron railing of a footbridge spanning the stream. I snapped a pensive moment of him sitting on the bank under a shady oak tree. He looked like a poet of yore. These photos are among the ones I treasure most. We took several shots of us posing on his back patio with the kitties. Later we took a spin over to Carlos O'Kelly's restaurant on Little River Turnpike near Fairfax City, and we enjoyed a wonderful dinner in the patio room. "Thanks for everything once again Mikey," I said gazing across the candlelit table at him wearing his faded jeans and a black tee shirt.

"My pleasure," he answered, clasping my hand.

The only cloud over the evening was when the waitress came by our table to take our order. She didn't mean to be rude but she glanced at my loose fitting blouse and must have jumped to conclusions because she smiled brightly and said, "Oh I see we have a table for three here tonight. Congratulations! And Happy Mother's Day!" Mike just laughed but I turned ten shades of scarlet and I vowed silently to do something about my expanding waistline. Being happy with Mike and enjoying his home-cooked meals was causing me to pack on the pounds. I sighed; my 40-something metabolism was not being cooperative with me.

In the middle of May, Michael and I accepted an invitation to the grand opening of a new restaurant located in Georgetown. The establishment was co-owned by an influential entrepreneur friend of Mike's and he wanted to show support. We left my house around 7:30 that evening, Mike handsome in a blue suit, I in my silky teal empire waist dress. Dad snapped a picture of us posing in the den and we made quite a contrasting pair, dusky and blonde. I felt very happy with his arm around my waist and he drove the Honda to Georgetown. We parked on a side road off M Street and Mike showed me his old friend Larry Mc Murtry's bookstore. It was fascinating to realize that he knew the famous *Lonesome Dove* author.

When we walked in the front door of the new establishment, it was nearly wall to wall people, most of them young enough to be our children! The music was blasting full volume, tunes I didn't know. My heart sank and looking over at Mike's face I could see his did too. Nonetheless, he robustly said, "Well here we are Rosy! Let's make the best of it. Let's go find a glass of beer and something to eat." We waded through the mob, pushing and being pushed until we finally got upstairs where we found a bartender with Michelob on tap. The nightclub was quite interesting with its railroad theme. It was decorated to look like an old depot inside and Mike and I took it all in, noting train memorabilia displayed on the walls and ornate lamps and benches.

"Look at all these people," Mike said, "All of them looking desperately for love, but none of them knowing anything nearly as wonderful as we do, Posy. We have the real thing!" I couldn't agree more.

After several hours of putting up with the noisy crowd and not really finding anything to eat besides some diminutive cocktail weenies, we decided we had had enough. Michael had imbibed a bit too heartily and I told him that I would drive home. He seemed disappointed but agreed. I took him on a short tour of Georgetown and Glover Park before we headed back toward Virginia.

We stopped at Mike's TV and Books and by then it was nearly two o'clock in the morning. The store looked very eerie in the dark shopping center, even when he switched the lights on. He put a tape he had made for this occasion on his old reel-to-reel Wollensak tape player and we sat back and relaxed, holding each other very tightly. I remember listening to old Beatles tunes, Eric Clapton, and "Inna Gadda Da Vida" by Iron Butterfly, the long version. At that juncture, he seemed mellow and a bit tired. "We better go to Roy's and get something to eat," I said nudging him gently as the tape ended.

"Ok honey," he answered, rising and stretching. When we pulled into the all night Roy Rogers drive-thru on Lee Highway in Arlington, I glanced over to ask Mike what he wanted to eat and was shocked! He didn't look well, his face a pallid, putty gray color almost cyanotic.

"Oh Mike baby! Are you all *right?*" I exclaimed.

"Sure Pudder, only kind of tired. I'll take a roast beef sandwich and a strawberry shake, please." I probably should have had him checked out at the Arlington Hospital ER but he insisted that he was fine, said it was likely just the harsh overhead fluorescent lighting. But earlier his face had looked ruddy if anything and this was such a contrast. We ate our sandwiches silently, both of us wishing we had left the Georgetown club earlier and had gone out to dinner at a nice family restaurant. I guess we were thinking how we were getting too long in the tooth to party hearty like we once did. We were geezers. That was a sobering thought. He left my house around four in the morning.

The next day was awful.

Mike called me from work right before Jo and I headed out to lunch. I was nursing a slight hangover, since I was no longer accustomed to drinking and I felt depressed about the night before, worried about Michael's unhealthy color and tiredness.

He didn't help matters by announcing, "Rosy, you know I've been thinking. Maybe your dad is right. The Honda might need major repairs. *It just might be a piece of crap after all!* I think the transmission could be shot. When I drove it last night I noticed that it didn't shift right. It seemed to hesitate when I changed gears!"

I was taken aback and groaned, "You're kidding! I just bought that car a little over a month ago and you assured me it was fine at the time!" I could feel anger rising inside me.

"Well you know it *is* a used car with 130,000 miles on it sweetie and you've got to expect these kinds of things to happen sometimes."

"Oh brother. How much is that going to set me back, a new transmission, Mike? Five hundred bucks?"

"No honey, more like $1500 at least."

"Fifteen **hundred!**" I shrieked, "Michael, did you know this when you had me buy the car?" He reassured me he knew no such thing but I was furious at that point, thinking he had taken me for a ride regarding the Honda.

"Jo and I are going out for lunch now. I'll talk to you later," I said stiffly as I dropped the phone.

I called him back later and he offered to buy the car from me or else split the cost for a new transmission. I suppose that should have appeased me but it only aroused my suspicions that he had known the car was a hunk of junk when he encouraged me to buy it! Maybe what my dad had said about the automobile was right; he had been giving me a hard time about it ever since I brought it home. Dad didn't like Japanese cars. We finally decided that the best thing to do with the Accord was to have it checked out by Mike's friends at the transmission shop on Friday that week.

"You know, I don't feel well today, Rosy. My heart hurts. My chest feels weird, almost like something has died in there or something."

I began to melt, suddenly feeling like a horrible harping witch for shouting at him.

"Mike you better see a doctor!"

"No, I'm just not up to partying like we did last night, I guess."

"Are you sure? You really didn't look too well at Roy's last night." I answered.

"Baby, I'm just getting old," he said with a slight chuckle.

The next night he came over to the house for my Dad's birthday party. He arrived waving an ornate ceremonial sword he had recently bought and gave Dad a funny cartoon card with the picture of a grinning, lecherous old man on the front. Inside it read "You're only as old as the women you feel." Dad was not amused. He started in on Mike about the Honda again and I sighed. *That damn car was going to break us up yet!*

"Dad, it's OK. We're having it checked out by the transmission people tomorrow. Who knows? It may be something simple and inexpensive to fix!" I said. He only grunted and uttered a curse word. The meal didn't go too well, as Mike seemed sullen and not himself. I think Dad's attitude really affected him. But at least his color looked good again, I saw to my immense relief. He left early as we watched *Mr. Holland's Opus* on video with our other guests. Around midnight Jo and I went to the 7 Eleven on George Mason Drive to buy some items and we noticed something in the road. It was a beautiful long-haired calico cat that appeared to be injured around her jaw area, possibly grazed by a car. We chased her off the road and cornered her beside a soft drink machine while we called Animal Rescue. As we waited for the animal caretakers, we talked to the poor kitty in soothing tones. She swallowed and looked up at us with huge, frightened eyes. After the county caught her in a net and transported her to the truck, we left. I hoped that they could eventually find her owner or a new home for her but I had my doubts. Still, what could we do? We couldn't just leave her in the road to get hit again! When we arrived home, I saw the answering machine light flashing urgently. Michael had left three messages, apologizing for acting unsociable at the party and asking me to call him back.

I returned his calls and told him about the cat. He sympathized for the poor animal and seemed relieved that Jo and I were home safe and sound. He was always concerned about my night owl hours.

"I'll see you tomorrow, Pee Wee. We'll take the car into the transmission place and see what's what," he said.

"Sure. Thanks for calling Mike. Love you," I signed off.

Chapter Eight

Distant Thunder

When we had the Honda inspected the next afternoon we were apprehensive as the mechanic drove us around in the car for a few blocks. It *was* hesitating quite noticeably as the automatic transmission shifted gears. We awaited his verdict with nervous hearts. "Actually this is a very simple problem to fix," he finally announced.

"How much will it be?" Mike asked.

"Oh, maybe thirty dollars or so," the man said, "Bring her in Monday morning, around nine and we'll adjust the shift points." Mike and I grinned at each other, ecstatic and overcome with relief. We celebrated with a huge Roy Rogers lunch.

The next week Miriam visited Mike's shop and we had a wonderful time, all three of us. Miriam looked quite attractive with her dark brownish hair neatly combed and makeup carefully applied. We laughed a lot and Mike seemed quite pleased with it all; I'd rarely ever seen him grin so broadly. His mom always tried to make a point of seeing him at least once a week, most often on Tuesdays. She'd drive her light blue Ford Taurus from her home in Northwest D.C. The Hardesty bunch always bought Fords, much like our family. Maybe it was a Midwest thing.

The rest of the month was fairly happy and we went out to eat quite a lot. Other times Michael cooked dinner for me. He was actually quite a chef when he put his mind to it and I enjoyed the candlelight, the cuisine, the chef and the service. He was spoiling me and I lapped it all up. Squeeky and Magic were always the other dinner guests on such occasions and we made quite a foursome.

Michael ended May by coming over for Memorial Day dinner. We had hamburgers grilled on our ancient hibachi. I burnt my fingers a bit while trying to remove a burger and put it on the plate. Although Michael was concerned about the injured hand, he seemed a little distracted. He left the table right in the middle of a conversation with Jo. It was not like him to show rudeness like that. He sat on the front steps with me, looking at old *Life* magazines he had brought over.

Later we three watched the movie based on Tennessee Williams' play, *This Property is Condemned* starring Natalie Wood and Robert Redford. After the film, we discussed the tragic story and got into a lively talk about Tennessee Williams, one of my favorite playwrights. Then Mike wanted to learn the rudiments of computer book searches so we spent nearly two hours going through the online book catalog. It's strange but I recall us searching the database of Amazon, which was only a fledgling online bookstore back in 1997, not the conglomerate of today. He seemed to catch on quickly despite being somewhat hesitant about computers in general. Before he left he handed me a humorous "five month anniversary" card to commemorate May 28th as he kissed me good-bye.

Jo's birthday was celebrated on June 6th that year instead of the usual 3rd day of the month because she had had her wisdom teeth pulled on her real birthday. We whipped up a little party with Ed and Mike. They had never really hit it off together before but that night we all watched the hilarious movie *The Birdcage* with Robin Williams and Nathan Lane. We four laughed so hard that our sides hurt.

On Father's Day I visited Mike's house and was surprised to see that his daughter Monica and her two boys, Kyle and Barry, were at the house too. We all went to Rutherford Park next door. Then we trekked to the nearby elementary school and played on the swings and slide like a bunch of overgrown kids. I took several pictures of Mike with his family. They left around seven and Mike and I ate our dinner and enjoyed a quiet evening together.

A few humid days later a severe afternoon thunderstorm was brewing over Bailey's Crossroads. There was electricity in the air, literally.

I called Mike on a whim, "Hey Mikey, a thunderstorm's coming up! Want me to come over to the shop?"

"Oh, you're darn tootin'!" he answered. I drove as quickly as I could, excited by the prospect of experiencing a tempest with him, watching the boiling green-gray nimbus clouds and lightning, shielded from the elements in his air-conditioned store. When I got there his face lit up.

"Pudder, I turned on all the sets to different stations to see the weather alerts!" Indeed he had: I saw Channel 4's Bob Ryan on one set, Channel 9's Doug Hill on another and some other weather broadcasters on the remaining TVs. We stared at the Doppler radar maps and looked out the large plate glass windows. The wind was howling and rain began to fall in sheets, punctuated by strobe-light bolts of lightning and crashing thunder. Traffic on Columbia Pike slowed to a crawl. We hugged each other, loving it. Both of us had a fascination with storms and joked about becoming "storm chasers" one day, in reference to those folks who follow tornadoes and other violent weather across the landscape. During the height of the tempest we went upstairs to the office building soda machine and bought a couple of soft drinks to sip while we viewed the natural fireworks. It all ended too soon but was exhilarating while it lasted.

Near the very end of June I spent a Sunday over at Mike's that will linger in my mind as one of the most peaceful ones we had ever experienced.

We didn't do much that day; it was too sultry for that. But we lay together on his bed, not making love or fooling around, just holding each other closely, eyes shut. Late afternoon sunlight dappled the room. The window was open letting the faraway voices of happy children from the local swimming pool filter into the room, a lazy, timeless sound that made me feel sleepy and happy. A very slight breeze played across our faces. Occasionally we heard the soft cooing of a mourning dove. I could have stayed that way forever I was so blissful. Michael kissed the top of my head and idly stroked my hair. "I really love you so much Rosy," he said.

"Same here," I countered. "Let's remember this forever."

"I was thinking the same thing."

Later that night, we looked at the half moon through a telescope that Michael had picked up earlier that month at the Salvation Army. Through the lens the orb gleamed silvery against the dark sky and you could make out craters and hills on the surface. Fireflies were just starting to blink their tiny green lanterns on and off and the sweet smell of honeysuckle perfumed the air. But the evening had to end. It was getting late and I had to drive home. We parted most reluctantly.

Time turned over the pages of the calendar to reveal July and I had high hopes for a wonderful summer spent with Michael. We had planned lots of things, including a trip to Harper's Ferry, West Virginia and a jaunt to Point Of Rocks, Maryland. Things started fortuitously with Independence Day spent in Manassas and watching *Picnic* at my house. After that weekend I went to Mike's shop mid-week, as was my custom, this time bringing with me *Coney Island,* a nostalgic Ric Burns and PBS's *The American Experience* video chronicling the defunct Brooklyn amusement park. He loved the old images on the film, being moved to tears by them. "We both love these old things so much, don't we Rosy?" he said, holding me tight. He had the lights turned off so we could view the film better and keep things cooler. Both of us enjoyed the movie but we were saddened and sickened by the part where the amusement park elephant named Topsy is electrocuted on camera. Mike was quite upset about the graphic footage of poor Topsy's demise.

The next Saturday he called me about the tortoise that he'd rescued from the road. Things were never the same after that.

We visited the doctor the Monday after our disturbing conversation at Green Spring. As I waited in the office while Michael was being examined I got into a conversation with several patients as we discussed old amusement parks, including Coney Island and our local Glen Echo and Marshall Hall. I walked over to the window of the fifth floor office and was amazed at the view from that perspective. One could see Seven Corners and the crowns of trees way off into the distant haze. The landscape looked like a pleasant series of gentle hills and no traffic was visible. After an hour or so Michael reappeared, a bit pale but he smiled at me and flashed the thumbs up sign. As he signed out with the receptionist he turned his back towards me and I gazed at the back of his neat, dark head. An almost maternal feeling of love washed over me, a fiercely protective emotion. Then without warning a foreboding overwhelmed me. ***"Mike's going to die!"*** I thought wildly, illogically. It was as if someone had suddenly cranked up the air conditioner in the building twenty degrees. I shuddered but he came over to me and we left the office and drove to a nearby diner at Spring Hill Motor Lodge to eat lunch. The pair of us had bacon and scrambled eggs with toast and grape jelly as we inspected his doctor's report. The EKG was good, as were other vital signs. His cholesterol was a little bit high and the physician had made a note saying he wanted to perform a few more tests on Michael. He was so relieved that the appointment was over that he chattered happily.

"I was scared to give blood, Rosy since I've never had it taken before but the nurse just talked to me, stuck the needle in and before I knew it, it was all over! God, I'm *starving*," he said, munching on a crisp slice of bacon. "I feel much better already. There's nothing wrong with my heart!"

In those early days, nobody thought of Michael's ailment as depression, since it seemed to be purely physical.

The first ominous rumblings of thunder on the horizon had occurred and this was one storm we were not going to enjoy.

Chapter Nine

Glimmer of Hope

Sometimes I awaken drenched in sweat, shaking off a nightmare in which I am trying to control my car but it seems to have a mind of its own. It suddenly reverses on me or speeds forward and I feel I am being hurled into dreaded oblivion. Other times in my nightmares I attempt to dial a number, choose a song on the jukebox or cry out to someone with all my might, calling their name endlessly. But my fingers dial the wrong number every time. I can never select the music I want to hear or worst of all, a scream comes out of my mouth completely silent. In small measure, these night terrors mirrored what was happening that summer with Michael.

The rest of that wildly erratic July melted down. We still had some fun times listening to music, talking, joking, walking in the park, all the things that people in love are supposed to do. But the magnificent afghan we had carefully knitted together was unraveling and both of us knew it. By August my boyfriend's symptoms had developed to such a degree that we felt powerless against the oncoming Tempest. The train was picking up speed and was threatening to derail. By the end of the month, we weren't really dating anymore but were spending our time together poring over weighty medical books, visiting doctors and the Fairfax Hospital ER as we tried to assimilate information about depression and male menopause.

Once in awhile Michael's former vibrant personality would reappear briefly and I became wildly hopeful, but just when it seemed that the man I loved would return to me, darkness would scurry in the room with a vengeance, like a horde of rustling, dirty roaches. We lamented the unfairness of it all, waiting our entire lives to find each other and then not being able to enjoy it.

As a finale, the discordant "Sorrowful Summer Symphony, Opus 55" reached a thunderous, strident crescendo and then... That treacherous, two-faced day, October 10, 1997 crashed into our lives. One of us went on. The other one was left behind.

The day the music died. Sudden silence, a terrible hush that seemed to still the songbirds in the trees.

The days immediately following the funeral were naturally the worst. I was a lost soul, stumbling around in a daze, waiting for a telephone call that would never come. I often wandered around my neighborhood at three o'clock in the morning, meandering aimlessly, staring at the sky and its cold, dazzling stars. I didn't care what happened to me. God didn't seem to care either. Even though I was not a Catholic, I could not forget how I had started a nine-day Saint Jude novena on October second. I had made a tiny cross mark on the kitchen calendar, October 10 when the novena was scheduled to end. In novenas you're supposed to say the prayer nine times a day for nine days. When your prayer is answered, you're honor bound to publish a thank-you note in the newspaper. I had prayed to Saint Jude several times before in my life and he had never failed me.

"May the Sacred Heart of Jesus be adored, glorified, loved and preserved throughout the world, now and forever. Sacred Heart of Jesus, pray for us. Saint Jude, worker of miracles pray for us. Saint Jude, helper of the hopeless pray for us. Amen." I whispered the last sentence of the novena around 8:30 on that dreadful morning...

(Another very odd thing happened at 8:30 that nightmare morning: There was a loud and terrible ruckus involving my two kitties, Snuggles and Sir Winston. Snuggles was eating at her food station

and it seems Winston snuck up on her, frightening her and her identification tag got caught in the plastic grill of the station, causing much caterwauling and an explosive noise as poor Snuggles broke away, with the grill still attached to her collar! Kibble was scattered everywhere on the kitchen floor.)

I found the utter stillness intolerable so I attempted to disrupt it by reading books written by fellow sufferers. Their brave stories about coping with unbearable loss touched my heart. Their experiences with loved ones contacting them from "the other side" caused a tiny firefly glimmer of hope to glow in my mind. *Maybe Mike's spirit, his personality, was not really dead at all!* Hadn't I sensed him walking beside me on October 10 at Long Branch Nature Center hours *before* I had even learned of his death? Perhaps he had merely shed his earthly attire and was now living in another "realm." After all, death is as much a part of life as birth. When I opened my mind a little to such possibilities, some very strange events began to occur in my life.

Barely two weeks after Michael's death I visited the Mary Riley Styles Library in nearby Falls Church. I often stopped by there because although it was small, it had a rich selection of books to borrow and an interesting collection of foreign videos that you could check out for a nominal fee. As you entered the front door, computer terminals displaying a Library Search function faced you. I normally paid no attention to these computers unless I was searching for a book myself. But this time I felt drawn to the foremost one. I walked over to it. Boldly lettered across the monitor screen were the words "The Portable Curmudgeon." I was dumbstruck; a few months before he died, Michael had loaned me that book! It was a slender volume of anecdotes compiled by Jon Winokur. It featured witticisms by famous "curmudgeons" like W. C. Fields, Groucho Marx, Dorothy Parker, H. L. Mencken, Fran Lebowitz, and many, many more. Their biting wit and observations about life always delighted Michael. I couldn't wait to tell Jo, who was sitting in the car outside the building.

That same week I visited the Arlington Central Library on

North Quincy Street. I was browsing through the self-help section when my eyes spied *Male Menopause,* a volume that I'd borrowed and loaned to Mike earlier that summer. On a whim I thumbed through the book. A business card fluttered to the floor. It was addressed to Mike and was from one of his customers! I was awe-struck. Apparently she had tried to stop by his shop and he had been closed so she'd left a note on her business card and had attached it to the outside of his store. He must have seen the card and then used it as a bookmark while reading the book, a common habit with him.

A few weeks later, Jo and I were returning home from the Styles library. We stopped at a traffic light in downtown Falls Church on Park Avenue, directly in front of the State Theatre. I was feeling very low and I wailed to Jo that Mike should give me another "sign" if he had really survived physical death and was now living in another dimension. I needed some comfort. The *Portable Curmudgeon* incident seemed long ago to me. My words to her had barely left my mouth when a large tanker truck entered the intersection from my right. As it rumbled through the light, Jo and I stared at it open-mouthed. In enormous letters painted on the side of the tanker was **"HARDESTY FUEL COMPANY."** *Hardesty was Michael's surname!* It's an uncommon name around Northern Virginia; there were only ten listings in the phone directory. We looked at each other in astonishment. So the old boy was up to something after all! I felt elated and I mentally thanked Mike for letting me see that sign.

Meanwhile, it appeared that Michael was making himself useful around the house. When he was on earth, he was quite handy at fixing things. He had a natural mechanical flair and he could diagnose a problem with ease and have some gadget repaired in no time flat. He took real pleasure in helping others. Jo was aware of this and one day she was vacuuming our dining room carpet. The hose of the machine was getting clogged, cutting drastically down on the suction. She tapped on the flexible pipe many times, made a makeshift coat hanger "awl" to try and prod the gunk out, and thumped the machine up and down repeatedly. She made no progress and after half an hour of this, she was angry and in despair. Sighing, she decided she would have to take the vacuum cleaner into the repair shop for an expensive fix. Jo put the canister vacuum down and went upstairs to take her morning bath, but before she did she impulsively asked Mike out loud, "Please Mike. Fix this damn thing!"

When she came downstairs later, she noticed a bright new quarter sitting on the dining room rug, right beside the hose. *It had not been there earlier.* That was shocking but even more stunning was how she turned on the vacuum cleaner and it now worked perfectly. This proved to be the first in an amazing series of "fix-its" that we attributed to Michael.

After his death, Marion and I gradually became good friends. It was a bit awkward at first since we had both dated Michael in the past and there was a natural tinge of jealousy to our relationship. We couldn't help but compare notes at times. But after awhile, we realized that we both had lots of ideals in common and we could understand what each other was going through in mourning Michael's passing. We shared a similar sense of humor and that pulled us through many a dark day. I told Marion about Mike's apparent "household helpfulness" and I convinced *her* to politely ask Michael for aid when an appliance went belly-up on her. She had an old TV set that he'd given her years before and it had stopped working completely some time earlier when a local transformer blew. Nothing could make that set come back on and she decided it was time to ditch it. Taking a cue from me, she too asked Michael for help with it. Not really expecting anything, she warily turned the knob. It came on instantly and worked flawlessly. In fact, it worked for many years after that. She was becoming a believer!

As a single woman, I found it comforting to have "a man around the house" but I didn't want to pester or disturb Michael if he indeed was being so helpful. Then a most comforting thought occurred to me. If he was responsible for these amazing "coincidences," then he must be OK wherever he was. He must not be in Hell or Purgatory after all! It seems that at last he had found some peace. For the rest of that dreadful autumn and winter of 1997, that thought kept me going.

I realize that these coping mechanisms may seem silly, whacko or out of touch to many people, but "you do what you gotta do" to get you through the night.

Some of the things that happened were actually quite humorous. One cold January morning my Dad had to be admitted to Arlington Hospital for several days with a stomach virus. When he parked in front of the hospital he left the headlights of his Ford Escort on by mistake and the battery was very dead when I drove by to check his car. I tried to get the little blue sedan to turn over but it refused; it would need a boost. It was after midnight and I joked out loud to Michael, "Well what are we going to do now, Mike?" I started to drive my own car home and had progressed five blocks from the building when I spotted a tow truck. What was painted on the side of the cab? "Mike's Towing" of course! The truck was from Maryland but when I looked up that business I could find no sign of such a place.

One of the hardest things about death is coping with a new reality. We can no longer just pick up the phone and call our loved ones to chat like we used to. It may take months to break the habit of rushing to the telephone every time it rings, expecting to hear the comforting voice we love so much. But I believe that in each soul's own unique way, they still "call us" often. Our contacts with departed loved ones usually appear as natural everyday events rather than those melodramatic special effects miracles portrayed in Hollywood Biblical epics. I have never noticed any thunder, lightning bolts, or heavenly choirs singing when I sensed Michael around but who knows? It would be very cool if one day that happened too! It's easy to overlook their help because it seems such a part of our day to day life. They still love us and keep their watchful eye on us to guide us through this difficult, painful world. Their personalities seem very similar to what they were on the earth plane. We in turn can help *them* by thinking kind thoughts about them and telling other people how special they were. We can pray for them too, which uplifts them wonderfully. It's a two-way street. Just like earth's inhabitants, they like to be told "I love you" frequently.

I can remember a reassuring event that happened on the first anniversary of Michael's death. Life is so filled with irritating, mundane details and death and taxes come to everyone. My Arlington County property tax decal for my car was quite late because the check was somehow misrouted and I was worried. Dad had been working on the problem day after day, making calls trying to straighten matters out. It was October 10, 1998 and I was most despondent. The past year had been so heart-wrenching that sometimes I was amazed I had even survived it. And yet here it was, a whole year later. In some ways I couldn't believe 365 days had passed since Black Friday but in other ways it felt like a century had transpired.

Mentally I communicated with Michael, telling him how much I missed him and loved him. I began to cry. The second I turned my mental radio onto my late boyfriend, Dad burst into the room waving an envelope. "Your car decal just came!" he shouted. I silently thanked Michael with all my heart.

While on earth, Mike always had been wary of people leaving checks or cash sitting about. He had chastised me on more than one occasion for being so cavalier with my money when he visited my home. It certainly was not safe, he pointed out; it was an open invitation for burglars. It seems he hasn't changed since crossing over. My Dad's sister Pat had generously given our family a check for six thousand dollars as part of a settlement on the estate of Dad's twin brother. I placed the check very carefully on the top of an antique French clock we have in our den. We've developed the habit of storing our mail there since it is convenient.

Apparently Michael did not approve because the next day I was horrified to find the check gone, no sign of it anywhere. I felt sick because Dad had told Jo and me that part of the money was ours. I intended to spend a portion of mine on something very special that I had wanted for a long time. Something I will tell about in a later chapter. But the money was *gone*. I was desolate. Tears welled in my eyes. A hunch told me to look *behind* the clock, which was not very close to the wall. Meticulously placed on the back of the timepiece, perfectly straight and lying flat against the metal was the check! How it stayed in place against the back and why it didn't simply flutter to the den floor, I'll never know. It was as if someone had painstakingly taped it to the clock with invisible adhesive. To please Michael I then put the check safely away in a drawer until it could be cashed.

Another time Jo, Dad and I tried with all our might to mount a heavy oven hood above our stovetop but it wouldn't cooperate despite our numerous attempts. We could barely lift it, much less line up the holes where the bolts were supposed to go. Huffing, puffing and dripping sweat, we gave up, arm muscles aching. Later that day I joked to Dad that we really ought to ask Michael to help us since we were as bad as The Three Stooges when it came to the unruly kitchen appliance. He said to ask Mr. Helpful Handyman for the heck of it. I did, saying out loud, "How about it Mikey? Think you could lend us a hand?" Instantly after that Dad and I alone were able to hoist the hood which suddenly seemed as light as the proverbial feather. It lined up perfectly and we hastened to bolt it into place on the kitchen wall.

Various household happenings have occurred so frequently over the years that I've become convinced that Michael is in a better world but he keeps his eye on this one as well. It's a most comforting thought and the evidence for this is difficult to ignore. Maybe it's hard to believe but *Michael has helped me every single time I have asked him.* He remains an easygoing fellow in the hereafter and I appreciate his aid more than I can ever say. He's truly a guardian angel. He's still Michael.

There was only one time that my request seemed to fall on deaf ears. It was July 5th, 2000 and perhaps I can remember the date so well because it was exactly three years earlier that Michael had paid his final visit to my house to watch the *Picnic* film. I'm odd about dates; they seem to stick in my memory for

CHAPTER NINE

the longest time. Recollections from long ago often spring unbidden into my mind on anniversaries of an event. At any rate, I recall that I lost my right earring on that day, a dainty silver and amethyst piece of jewelry that Michael had liked very much. I searched every inch of the house for it, the yard and even Westover shopping center but it was lost forever. Every day I mentally asked for Michael's assistance in finding it, but every day I was disappointed. Two weeks went by and still no earring. I told Jo and Marion that this was the first time Mike had not responded. I tried to shrug it off but inside I felt blue.

I realized that I bothered the poor man far too often and I felt truly guilty about it. Coping with his death and losing such an important part of my life was a big hurdle for me to overcome. Other women still had their husbands and boyfriends on earth, flesh and blood men who were there to comfort and hold them, to help and reassure them. I longed for that too but I couldn't find anyone who could measure up to Michael. I sought the same solace as they did but I had to approach it in a different way and sometimes I felt like such a whiney, demanding battle-ax. At times I was convinced that Michael was thoroughly sick of me. Other times, I thought I had truly gone around the bend with the grief of it all.

It was July 19th and Jo was having vacuum cleaner trouble… again. She pulled the full, dirty, bag out and was going to throw it in the trash when something stopped her. She said we needed to look inside the receptacle. She'd never made such a request before. It was disgusting to open up, filled with cat hair, birdseed, dust, paperclips, fuzz and dry cat food. We searched through the mess, pulling up handfuls of gunk and sifting through it, nearly choking from the grime. We saw nothing and she pulled the trash bin over so we could throw the bag out. I decided to plunge my hands in the middle of the rubbish one final time. Something gleamed silvery in the kitchen light and I pulled it out, examining it closely. My lost earring! Michael had come through after all, God bless him.

Chapter Ten

Double Heartbreak

Death is never easy to face but when two tragedies strike within days of each other the pain is nearly intolerable. This was Michael's mother Miriam's lot. After hearing about Michael's suicide, Miriam's husband Charles collapsed and became very ill. On October 15th, the day before Michael's funeral I called Miriam and asked her if she needed a ride to the ceremony, knowing that she drove infrequently at that point in her life.

"Hi Miriam. How are you? And how is Charles doing today?" I asked

"Charles is in the hospital, Rosy. They think he might have pneumonia! He was so upset over Mike that he got real sick," she answered.

"Oh dear! The bad news never stops, huh? Please tell Charles that I hope he feels much better soon. Tomorrow is Mike's funeral service at Quantico. Are you planning on going? It's at noon, I think."

"I wish I could but I don't think I could drive that far and I don't know the way."

"If you like, I can give you a lift, Miriam. I am going to try to go. Don't know if I'll make it all the way or not though."

"Thank you Rosy, I appreciate that but I guess I better stay here with my husband. He might need me and he seems so sick. He *is* almost eighty years old, you know. I'll have to be ready to go to the hospital at any time. But I expect he'll be better soon. He needs me now more than Mike does. I wish I could go though, for Mike's sake," she said.

"Well, I'll be thinking about you Miriam," I said, "Will Mike's brother Tom be there do you think?"

"Oh I doubt it. I don't think he can take time off from the newspaper. But I'll be thinking about Mike tomorrow anyway."

"I'll let you know how it all goes, OK?" I said, feeling on the verge of another crying jag thinking of the upcoming service.

"Ok. Thanks again Rosy," she concluded.

When I called her up the next day, after Mike's funeral was over, she had some more sad news. At first it appeared that Charles merely had a bad cold or pneumonia but after careful testing, doctors determined that he needed open heart surgery as soon as possible. Miriam had high hopes for the operation's success and was busily preparing the house for his homecoming. Like her son, she was also a "cat person." Her two big tabby boys, brown Stripes and creamy orange TomTom anticipated the return of "papa" too.

"I sure hope they don't get so excited when Charles comes in the front door that they trip him up, the way Nonny did me, some years ago!" she chuckled, "I hurt my ankle tripping over that kitty, after we came back from Sugar Loaf Mountain."

"Oh I hope not!" I said, "But they will be glad to have their daddy back home, to spoil them to pieces."

She said that surgery was scheduled for him very soon. I didn't say anything to her but I had misgivings about a man of Charles's age having open-heart surgery. When the day of the operation arrived, she told me that everything was ready for his homecoming; the house was tidied up and the little guys were all brushed and clean. They kept running up the stairs to the front door every time they heard it open.

But it was not to be. On October 30, 1997 Charles passed away on the operating table.

Miriam and I consoled each other throughout the darkest days and I'm forever thankful to her for being such a supportive friend. In many ways she reminded me of Michael. The same laconic Iowa wit, her love of creatures and even her speech inflections were similar to his. Mike had told me on several occasions that Miriam and he had been great friends, besides being related. He called her a "smart cookie." Before she had suffered a crippling aneurysm that had put her into a coma for weeks, several years previously, she had been a brilliant and sparkling personality. The two of them had enjoyed lively debates and intellectual discussions about philosophy, politics and many other subjects. Like him, she had been a voracious reader. He even called her one of his favorite people in the whole world.

We both missed Mike so much that our talk naturally turned to the subject of him. When we spoke almost daily on the phone we laughed and we lamented but eventually our talk turned to the possibility of an afterlife. She was unsure about such a thing and believed that she'd find out when she got there. I was a bit more convinced of the concept and I enjoyed telling her about the latest "Mikey sighting." She would always chuckle when I related something unusual that had occurred in connection with her son.

In fact some rather remarkable things happened between Miriam and me. Since we both were enamored with felines, most of these events involved our cats. The first occurred on December 28, 1997, a year to the day when Michael first came to my house to perform at the Christmas party.

Miriam owned the aforementioned Stripes and TomTom but she also fed another kitty she christened "Brother." Brother was a bit like Stripes and the two of them were the same age and first appeared at her house together several years earlier. She assumed that Stripes and Brother were probably littermates. The smoky gray tomcat was always skittish and would never enter the house but he did appear like clockwork for a nightly handout outside her sliding basement door. He disappeared on December 14th and Miriam was increasingly worried about him since the street next to hers carried quite a lot of traffic.

When the 28th arrived, I was feeling quite glum, thinking back on that happy night, now lost to time and I sympathized with Miriam's concern about the missing cat. I think the first year after a death invariably brings up "anniversary" recollections. I decided to try something. Out loud I asked, "Mike, I know you must remember this day, a very important one for us. Please show me you still care and can remember our time together. It's our anniversary, for God's sake! And please let Miriam find her kitty too. Thanks. I love you!" The plea was barely out of my mouth when Mike's mother called and reported that the errant Brother had *just shown up* at the back door, hungry for his dinner! I was amazed at how quickly Michael seemed to respond.

A nearly identical episode happened with my tabby and white cat Snuggles the following summer. She was very elderly and thin and she had disappeared for a day and a half during a horrid August heat wave. I made "Wanted" posters, tacked them up on the nearby telephone poles and was frantic with worry. On top of that, my Florida cousins chose that day to pay a visit. I felt very distracted and fretful but I didn't let on to my relatives. They departed around four in the afternoon and after they left, exhausted, I went upstairs to take a nap. The tears started rolling down my face as I thought of poor Snuggles probably dying of thirst out in the ruthless heat. I remembered what had transpired with Brother the previous December so I asked Mike out loud for help with finding Snuggles. He had always liked her himself.

Once again, the supplication was barely out of my mouth when the phone rang. I dashed to Mom's room to answer it and a lady's voice said, "Do you have a cat named Snuggles? I found her and she's here in my house!" It seems that the woman, who lived across traffic-snarled Lee Highway, had seen a strange kitty in her back yard and she'd been able to get close enough to read the tag attached to her collar. She hadn't even noticed the "Wanted" posters mounted on poles nearby. She coaxed Miss Snugs into her kitchen and called me promptly.

Unbelievably, this happened a third time. After the incident with Snuggles, we kept our cats indoors. Despite this, my old black, diabetic cat Sir Winston somehow sneaked out. He needed daily insulin and food to keep his body from going into shock. An entire day passed and it was getting close to dark. I sat on the brick garden wall and couldn't help sobbing. My cats were like children to me and my Winston had such a brave heart. He had battled against impossible odds in the past and survived, conquering diabetes, heartworm, liver disease and acute kidney failure.

Once again, I asked poor Michael for help! I got up after pleading with him and walked around the house. As I rounded the corner to the back yard, Dad suddenly opened the screen door and began yelling: "Now hear this! Now hear this! Sir Winston has officially arrived!" Then I heard Jo 's happy voice calling, "Here kitty kitty!" Much to my surprise, pudgy Winston was waddling up to the back step, hungry for supper.

Many times when I was feeling especially blue, Miriam would call me the next minute and cheer me up. She seemed to know when things were the blackest. One time was particularly striking. I was lying on the basement couch with headphones on, listening to oldies on the radio. "Unchained Melody" one of Mike's all time favorites was playing. Tears began to flow (I know...again! Would they ever stop??) as I felt a pain down deep in my soul. I missed Michael so much that I only wanted to die, to be with him once more. I found myself communicating a prayer to him. "Please Mike. Let me know you're here. I don't know what to do with my life. I'm trying to deal with your leaving but it's *so dreary here on earth!* Please give me a little sign that you're still here with me in spirit. Please tell me you still love me." Unbelievably, the phone rang then. A quick glance at my digital watch dial told me that it was 4:25 in the morning! I got up to answer the telephone, thinking it was a wrong number or a crank call. But it was Miriam! She had awoken and had heard *her* phone ring and thought it was *me*. We talked for a few minutes and then Miriam grew sleepy and we rang off. I felt truly awed and infinitely better. I thanked Michael for being there after all.

Perhaps one of the eeriest incidents with Miriam happened in December 1997 after my sister and I had visited Manassas,

Virginia before Christmas. The Fourth of July with Michael was the last time I'd been there and memories overwhelmed me. The quaint town looked truly beautiful, all decorated for the holidays. A freight train was stopped for a long time in the middle of Old Town, near the depot. I was idly thinking of how unsafe it would be for a person to scoot under one of the boxcars or hopper cars, even if the train was stopped like that. No telling when the locomotive might re-start. Another idea entered my head as well, actually more of an image. I could vividly picture Michael in a graduation cap and gown for some reason. I'd never seen a photo of him like that but I was trying to imagine what he might look like. Very cute, I decided.

Later that night Miriam called. Without any prompting from me, she told me an anecdote about how she and her brother Bud had once walked to school in an Iowa snowstorm. A train was stopped in town, blocking their path to the schoolhouse. Bud was on the point of scurrying under one of the cars when the train moved! He pulled back in the nick of time. I was shocked because I hadn't even mentioned the Manassas freight train to her yet.

But there was more. She went on to tell me that she'd been cleaning house all day. In her tidying up she had come across a picture of Michael that she'd forgotten she even owned. A spooky chill went through my body as I asked her to describe the photo. "Well he has a graduation cap and gown on," she began, "And he's real cute!"

The winter months passed and for the most part Miriam seemed to be coping remarkably well despite her double loss. Naturally she was quite depressed at times but she managed to take care of her financial affairs and to look after her cats. She'd withdrawn money from half a dozen bank accounts and planned to consolidate the funds into one central account. I talked to her on a Tuesday night in early February 1998 and she was very upbeat. She'd been examined by her doctor and was proclaimed fairly fit. Miriam joked that she might even live as long as her mother who died at ninety-one. Her birthday was the coming week and I had a few gifts I intended to give her. She was taking care of business and I admired her fortitude.

But the next day was icy and the roads were slick. The boys were out of cat food and she had to shop at the grocery store to replenish the larder. I didn't know this when I called her repeatedly and fruitlessly that Wednesday. It was like Michael all over again, the panic, the worry, and the bad news. Two days later I found out she'd slipped and fallen in the store and had been hospitalized. But in the meantime, nobody had any idea what had happened to her and I was very upset, fearing that her car might have skidded on the ice and fallen in a ditch or that she might have been abducted or...worse.

By Thursday night I was feeling extremely unhappy. As I sat on my living room sofa in the dark, without provocation a vivid scene flashed into my mind. I could suddenly "see" Michael's house inside especially his living room. It was quite unnerving as I felt like I was almost there, so clear was the detail. It was very strange indeed. The next day Dad suggested that we might want to drive out to Michael's former house, rationalizing that maybe Miriam had driven there for reasons of her own. It made as much sense as anything else I'd heard at that point and remembering the previous night's eerie experience, I drove out there with Jo. The house appeared dark and silent, illuminated only by a front porch light. I knew that many of his books, prints, and other collectibles were still sitting in the house, awaiting auction at an upcoming estate sale. The day was cold, morose and rainy and right away I noticed something odd about Michael's garage door. *Someone had jimmied the door open and had broken in!* The doorknob was completely off the door. My heart leaped as I imagined that Miriam might be in there, being held hostage perhaps. It all seemed most sinister, coupled with her vanishing act two days earlier.

Next I did a very foolhardy thing. I left Jo in the car and cautiously crept inside the garage (which Michael had converted to a spare room years earlier) and then into the kitchen and living room. The house was quiet except for the dismal drip, drip, drip of the February rain outside. Everything looked melancholy in the gray afternoon light filtering through the kitchen window and front door panes. I saw one of Michael's original abstract paintings hanging prominently on the wall leading to upstairs. Somehow it startled me to see it. Oddly enough, the raw coldness from the day didn't seem to penetrate the interior. It was warm inside, *as if someone had recently broken down the door!* I thought I could hear some sort of faint, soft, rustling or slithery sound, almost like pliable cloth brushing against something, and my scalp prickled. I needed to get out of there *fast!* I sensed an overwhelming feeling of sadness and creepiness. Before I left, I glanced one last time at his living room and I was struck by how much it looked like the "vision" I'd had of it the night before.

In near panic I raced to Mike's daughter's workplace to tell her of the break-in and my continuing fears about Miriam's disappearance. I waited for several anxious moments until I talked to Monica. Then I melted with relief when she told me some good news. It seems Miriam was in the hospital and was doing OK. Monica thanked me for informing her about the burglary and I went home, feeling much better. I suspect that Michael was relieved too since he wouldn't have wanted anyone breaking in.

While Miriam was hospitalized, her cats needed care. My sister and I volunteered to drive to her house near Carter Barron Amphitheatre in Northwest, D.C. to feed and water her babies and change their litter pans. We shopped at SuperFresh and brought lots of moist food, dry Friskies, litter and small garbage bags for them. The pair was shy at first but soon warmed up to Jo and me. I visited Miriam in the hospital after that and told her that the kids were all right. She seemed relieved to hear it although she desperately wanted to go home. She'd been through enough heartache and merely wanted to return to her beloved cats. Only animal lovers can understand the unbreakable bond between pet and owner, especially during trying times. When we suffer, they suffer and vice versa.

As fate would have it, Miriam was hospitalized for nearly a month and when she was released to her home she was never really the same. She could no longer drive and had a part-time day nurse to look after her needs. By that time, I'd adopted her two cats and in addition to my own three cats, I now owned five! It was a bit overwhelming at times but our family grew to love Stripes and TomTom. Because Miriam could no longer care for them properly the poor souls were fated to be put down unless I took them in. There never was any doubt in my mind that I would adopt them. I talked about the cats to Miriam on the phone as often as I could and I sent her some photos of the babes in their new home. But as 1998 limped on, it was obvious that Miriam was getting more despondent and giving up hope. My efforts to cheer her up didn't seem to work. She was tired all the time and not interested in life. We did have a wonderful conversation on Independence Day, almost like old times but she went downhill after that and she died on the exact same day her husband had a year earlier. I missed her terribly.

But apparently Miriam was not really finished. A funeral service was arranged at her home on November 5, 1998. Robin and Monica planned to scatter her ashes about her back yard among her flowers and the graves of her departed kitties — she had owned over forty in her lifetime! It was the night before the service and I had driven to the drugstore to get some medicine to settle my queasy stomach; I seemed to have a touch of intestinal flu and doubted that I could attend Miriam's service the next day. I felt unhappy, letting her down like that. As I was driving home along Lee Highway in Arlington an idea struck me. I asked Miriam out loud, "Hi Miriam. I hope you're doing OK over there. I miss you! And I hope you understand that I might not make it to your service tomorrow. The thing I want to know is, have you met Mike over there? Have you two reunited? If so, please give me some kind of sign!" I knew that she had always spoken with hope about reuniting with Mike someday. I couldn't believe it. My words trailed to nothing as I witnessed *blink *blink *blink *blink *blink! Five streetlights along the highway that were unlit for some reason came on in rapid succession one right after another. They winked on as soon as I drove past each one. Everyone knows that occasionally a streetlight or two acts strangely but five in a row like that? The odds seem stacked against such a possibility!

I tried one other "test" to see if Miriam was still aware of me left behind on earth. A few months later, I asked her once again to show me a portent that she and Mike had met up on the other side. I requested her to send me the names Michael and Miriam together to indicate such a thing. Then I went to check my email. Imagine my surprise when I saw a letter from a friend of mine named Michael and he mentioned the name Miriam in that letter!

1998 was drawing to a close and I made the decision to write to Mike's brother Tom in Sigourney, Iowa in mid-November. We bonded right from the start and eventually he made the long trek by car to our home on two separate occasions. During the visits we all had a great time, including Dad who loved to talk about Iowa and Mom, who loved Tom's keyboard playing. We became very close friends and pen pals over the ensuing years. Tom was a huge source of comfort to me. He and Mike had a boyhood friend named Pete and we became friends with him and his lovely wife Hazel as well. We welcomed visits from Pete and Hazel and looked forward to hearing the latest Iowa news.

Mike's brother had many personality traits in common with him. They were such delightful, caring people and so interested in partaking of the banquet of life: lofty ideas, music, art, poetry, ballet, vintage films, literature, architecture, history, photography, philosophy, etc.

But, they also shared the same sadness deep in their souls and they battled the Black Dog of depression. Tom too passed by his own hand on October 30, 2004. Two of my best friends had left me behind...

Not only was Tom a gifted musician and photographer but he was also a writer and poet. This is a touching poem that Tom wrote for his little brother Mike:

"Prayer for My Brother

    Mike was my little brother,
    He always was my little brother
    and he always will be.

    Oh, Great Spirit,
    My little brother stands before you
    to make an account for himself.

    Shine down your blessings on him
    now as always.

    Help us to be ever mindful of
    the greatest blessing of them all
    in this life-

    When the dawn breaks on a new day
    and the bright sun shines on everything.

    Let a new day dawn for Michael, too,
    Great Spirit, I do ask,
    by keeping memories of him alive
    deep in our hearts."

Chapter Eleven

The Art of Recovery

1998 was an unrelentingly dreary year, no matter how you look at it, especially after the death of Miriam. My routine life around the house continued, caring for my mother and other various duties and chores that sapped my spirit. When I had been with Michael I felt incandescent with life and energy. When he departed he took all the color and zest out of the world for me. I felt like a dispirited old drudge. Sometimes I wondered what I'd done so wicked that I deserved such a fate. Other times I felt like a middle-aged Cinderella without her Fairy Godmother or Prince Charming.

One positive aspect that emerged from this negative period was my growing interest in creating 3D artwork on my Dell computer. I'd purchased some graphics software called "Bryce 3D" and it had opened new vistas for me art-wise. With Bryce I could envision a scene in my mind's eye and bring in various models or meshes to create the setting. These models ranged from buildings, furniture, cars and trees to virtual figures. After the models were imported I could add precisely the amount of light I wanted and simulate any time of day or night. I could position the virtual camera in any position, like a Hollywood movie director in miniature. In Bryce one can add realistic-looking "water" to the environment, water that shows all the proper reflections and color of the real liquid. One can even move "mountains" in the program! It was fascinating and I found myself putting aside my acrylics, pen and ink, pencils, calligraphy pens and other traditional art media for this new one. You might say I was hooked.

While waiting for a 3D scene to render (paint) to the screen, you can twiddle your thumbs as it can take an hour or more depending on how complicated your object materials are. I was rather bored one night around nine o'clock as I stared at the monitor, render in progress. My unoccupied mind suddenly was filled with the name "Chuzzlewit," one of Michael's former cats. He had named the kitty after Charles Dickens's *Martin Chuzzlewit* and when the animal sneezed, Mike said it sounded like that word! Curious name, I thought. Around eleven, I went to Hollywood Video to peruse their selection. Nothing looked interesting until I spotted an old movie called *Our Miss Brooks*, starring Eve Arden. I'm a fan of vintage films and this one looked pretty good, judging by its cover case.

I watched part of it, buttered popcorn tub in hand. Miss Brooks was tutoring a reluctant student and she was ready to give him his homework assignment. I nearly choked on my popcorn and Big Gulp when she told him to *"read Martin Chuzzlewit and make a report about it."* There are thousands of videos in that store and I had unknowingly picked one with that name in it!

Something equally unprecedented happened at a later date. When Michael was on earth, synchronicity was important to him and he treasured odd little coincidences, as I mentioned before. He sometimes looked upon the phenomena as a game and I reasoned that he must not have changed much by crossing over. At that point I was 100% convinced that Michael did still exist in another dimension. There were far too many strange occurrences to attribute them merely to "chance." It was a major step in my recovery from grief to acknowledge his continued survival.

In a teasing mood, I played a mental game with him. I asked him to send me some sort of reference to his favorite philosopher, Arthur Schopenhauer, within the next month. This sign about Schopenhauer could appear in any context, whether on the Web, magazines, newspapers, as long as I did not seek it out purposely; that would be cheating on my part. The month wore on and no sign. I was a little miffed but I assumed it was entirely too difficult for him to accomplish.

I assumed wrong.

It was in early December and I needed some fancy gold-lined envelopes for my Christmas cards. I visited Michaels Arts & Crafts Store at Seven Corners Shopping Center and didn't find what I wanted. Even though holiday traffic was heavy I decided to drive a couple miles further to Borders Books in Bailey's Crossroads. They might carry envelopes there, I reasoned. I hadn't shopped at that store for several years and it wasn't on my way home. When I arrived at Borders I checked the front of the bookstore where gift items are featured but was disappointed. A sudden prompting sent me hurrying to the very back of the book section where psychology books seemed to be shelved. I didn't stop to browse a single book. Finally I reached the rear of the vast store. Not fully realizing what I was doing, I impulsively reached up on a shelf and grabbed a thick black book with white lettering. To my astonishment the book was about suicide and it naturally opened to a page as I placed it in my hands, spine against my left palm. On the footnote at the bottom of that opened page was the name "Arthur Schopenhauer!"

Many bereaved people report hearing a loved one's favorite song playing unexpectedly on the radio. They take this as a sign that the person is still in their presence. I think they're right. This "musical miracle" had happened numerous times when I drove past the building where Michael's shop once was. Such songs as Dusty Springfield's "I Only Wanna Be with You," "Unchained Melody" by the Righteous Brothers, B.J. Thomas's "This Time The Girl Is Gonna Stay," Deana Carter's "And We Danced Anyway" and "Every Day" by Buddy Holly. Michael loved these songs and played them on his guitar often. He also dearly loved the old Cascades song "Rhythm of the Rain." Jo and I drove past his birthplace on Reservoir Road in the Palisades section of the District (now The Lab School) one afternoon and that song began to play at the exact moment we rounded the corner. It came on so frequently when we drove past his old shop that we lost count.

There is a beautiful but obscure Everly Brothers tune originally written by Paul McCartney. It's titled "On the Wings of a Nightingale." I heard it on the radio for the first and only time back in 1984 when Jo and I were driving to Pope's Creek, Maryland, but never heard it again. Years later, the last time I visited Mike's shop a week before he died, a customer brought in an Everly Brothers album featuring that tune. Mike bought the album from the person and we played the song on his turntable. Because I liked it so much he gave the album to me.

Fast-forward ahead several years to a rainy afternoon at Applebee's in Falls Church. Ed, Jo and I were meeting there for lunch. We were sipping our beers and sodas and were waiting for our food. The neighborhood bar & grille was quite crowded and noisy. Jukebox music played in the background. I struggled to listen to a song that was playing and sounded oddly familiar to me. Then it hit me. It was "On the Wings of a Nightingale." I hadn't heard that song anywhere except my home stereo since that last time at Michael's. That was bizarre enough but with a shiver I realized something else. Applebee's was built on the former site of The Boar's Head, a restaurant Michael frequented all the time years before we met.

It seemed natural to me that a music lover like Michael would express himself frequently through that medium and music *is* known as the "universal language" after all. In another incident a line from the REO Speedwagon song "I Can't Stop This Feeling Anymore" started playing in my head, out of the blue. I liked the words so much that I considered varying them a bit and using them in the Michael memorial tribute I placed in *The Washington Post* each October 10. "Like a candle in the window on a cold dark winter's night" was the line that stuck. I decided that I might as well ask Mikey for approval as to whether he liked it too. I figured if I heard that song play on the radio that day, then that would be his stamp of approval.

When dealing with the alternate dimension one doesn't have ideal communication, but a type of telepathic shorthand seems to be the name of the game. Later that evening the song indeed did play on the car radio as I drove home from nearby Merrifield. But the story didn't end there. A couple weeks later Jo heard a squawking commotion coming from our cockatiels in the dining room. She had turned on the boom box earlier to entertain the birds. As she opened the door to the room the FM radio sang, "Like a candle in the window on a cold dark winter's night." The exact part of the song I had chosen! Or rather Mike had chosen...

Not only can music be a way of communicating from the hereafter but TV, magazines, books, movies and the Internet can also be a conduit to their energy. Try to imagine for a moment that *you* are the one who has passed on. How would *you* go about getting a message back to your loved ones left behind? You would want to tell them not to mourn your passing. You would want to tell them that you're in a beautiful, happy place and you still love them very much and are waiting for the day they join you forever. You would probably use any means at your disposal to telegraph the word. It would be frustrating at times when your loved ones ignored the communications that you worked so hard to send. And it might be equally frustrating when your friends left on earth pestered you for too many signs!

I admit I was guilty of the latter. It was such a thrill to receive word from Michael that I looked forward to each sign like a wonderful gift from him. It made me feel close to him, almost like when he was here on earth. A playful idea came to me. Mike and I had enjoyed immensely Robert Klein's comedy album "Child Of The 50's." I "asked" Mike to let me see Robert Klein somewhere that week, the name or the man himself in the media. Later that night I got very sleepy and tried to take a nap on the living room couch, but the sofa was lumpy and uncomfortable and I couldn't drift off. I was tired and rather bored so I grabbed the local TV guide. My eye fell on Bill Maher's show

"Politically Incorrect." One of the guest listed for the November 8th show was...Robert Klein. I could almost hear Michael's snicker and I grinned too.

Chapter Twelve

What a Tangled Web We Weave

The World Wide Web is so pervasive these days that nearly everyone, no matter how remote his or her location, can log on to it and communicate. One day I expect to see an otherworldly URL: www.otherside.com. As distinguished a scientist as Thomas Edison was working on a device to communicate with departed ones when he died. Rumor has it he was nearly finished with the machine. I've always believed that if the phenomenon of after-death communication was valid then it probably could be measured scientifically and harnessed to create a "ghost telephone" or "spirit TV." Even though applied science has made great strides in the past two hundred years, there is still much about the electromagnetic spectrum we don't really understand.

My admittedly unscientific theory is that souls who pass on communicate with us through electromagnetic waves of a certain frequency. Perhaps these waves are too low frequency or high frequency for most of our ears but animals seem to detect them with their superior hearing capability and children sometimes do too. Certain psychics might have this enhanced hearing ability. I suspect ESP, mental telepathy and clairvoyance operate on similar wavelengths. That might explain why we often "feel" or "sense" our loved ones around without actually seeing them as an image with our eyes or hearing their voices with our physical ears. There could be an area in the brain that is sensitive to such "vibrations."

In the years following Mom's illness and confinement, Jo and I found ourselves unable to venture forth too far afield. No more late night parties in Georgetown or vacations of any sort. As she became more feeble and helpless, our duties only multiplied. Our "real" social life, outside of Ed's visits, became nearly non-existent so we naturally turned to the Net for companionship. We acquired a number of "virtual" friends that we have grown remarkably close to over the passing years; they seem like family members and Jo and I love every one of them. The emoticon became our apprentice in portraying our moods :-). At first it all felt very artificial but today emailing friends is as natural as breathing.

For better or worse, I consider myself quite a computer geek and I surf the Web frequently and belong to YouTube, Facebook and Twitter. On the other hand, Michael knew surprisingly little about computers. He didn't really trust the machines and preferred low-tech pastimes like reading books and writing with pen and paper. He still typed on an old manual Underwood. He thought that computers might insidiously suck their users into a virtual world from which it would be difficult to escape. On summer nights we would saunter around his neighborhood and every house had the ubiquitous phosphorescent glow of a computer monitor in its window.

"Just look at that Rosy!" he'd say, "Not a soul out walking on a nice night like this. Nobody even sits on their front porches anymore, they're so hooked on their computers and video games." It *was* rather eerie and I could see validity in his aversion to the gadgets. Over the past several years I've cut back on my own computer time and have rediscovered joy in simpler old fashioned pastimes like sketching with pencils, reading actual books, playing the keyboard, walking and sky watching on starry nights.

No matter how Michael felt about computers while he was on the earthly plane, he seemed to use them for communications from the hereafter. Occasionally Jo was the one who discovered these clues since she was on the Web far more often than I was. The first hint of this was when Jo and I admired the artwork of an artist named John Martzahn who uploaded his creations to America Online's Graphic Arts Community under the name "BeyondVR." She emailed the artist telling him how much she enjoyed one of his pieces. According to his profile, this person lived in Davenport, Iowa. He was pleased with the praise and Jo wrote to him one more time with an improbable question. Since he was from Iowa, did he know anybody from the little town of Sigourney? AOL had a worldwide membership of 18 million users at the time and the question seemed very farfetched, plus Iowa is a fairly large state.

Imagine our astonishment when he wrote back that he knew some people named Hardesty who were originally from that town! The full story turned out to be even *more* incredible than at first glance. It seems BeyondVR grew up three blocks away from Michael's nephews Paul and Richard. He was a very close friend with both boys throughout his youth and he had many a story to tell about adolescent escapades.

In another strange incident, an online pal once told me about a duet by Aaron Neville and Linda Ronstadt called "Please Remember Me." She believed that for some reason Michael wanted me to be familiar with the song. I'd never heard it before she brought it to my attention but I enjoyed the song when I listened to it online. It was Valentine's Day 2002 and I felt very low. As I mentioned earlier, that romantic holiday back in 1997 was magical when Michael had surprised me with a big bouquet of flowers, a well-stocked candy box covered in pink roses, and mushy cards. He serenaded us for hours with his guitar in accompaniment to our keyboards and Ed's rich baritone. But here it was February 14, 2002 and the holiday fell flat. It was a sobering thought to realize that all those years had passed and I still hadn't found any man to fill Michael's shoes. But I'd made up my mind that I'd rather go solo than waste time on someone who wasn't right for me. Sometimes a feeling comes along once in a lifetime.

On Valentine's Night, I visited my favorite store, Ayers Hardware in Westover to pick up some things. I parked out front, made my purchases and headed out the *back* door instead of the front. I don't know why I did that because my car was in the front. As I walked through the store I heard the sound system playing a song. Against all odds, it was "Please Remember Me" by Aaron Neville and Linda Ronstadt! If I'd exited by the front door I never would have heard it. I guess Michael remembered it was Cupid's holiday after all.

When you think of it, you get confirmation nearly every day in many different ways that your loved ones on earth still love you. They call you, invite you to lunch or dinner, take the kids to soccer practice, do the dishes when you are dead tired, leave love notes on your pillow, hold your hand, or kiss you tenderly; they telegraph "I love you" in countless actions, words and gestures. Just because someone has "passed on" doesn't mean that you automatically stop missing all this attention. At least I certainly missed it with Michael and I sometimes invented "mind games" that I would play with him.

In one of these instances, Internet serendipity came into play yet another time. "Casey Jones" the engineer was something I challenged Michael to come up with one month. As I mentioned earlier, he used to dress up as Casey and had his name on his vanity license plate. It's remarkable how clicking on one website leads to another one, in ever expanding circles like the ripples in a pond. I was cleaning out my "Favorite Places" folder and was testing the addresses to make sure they were still active. I clicked on a virtual pet cemetery site where folks posted photos and poems dedicated to their cherished animal friends. In one of the "plots" was an ode to a cat named Casey Jones!

Miriam had never used a computer as far as I knew but somehow that didn't stop one of her kitties — yes you heard me right, her *kitty* — from getting his "meowssage" across. Since Miriam had passed away, our family had really taken to Stripes and TomTom. Because we'd forged such a strong bond with them, we felt great sadness that we lost TomTom to hyperthyroidism in May 2000. He died right before our eyes on the kitchen floor while the vet was treating him. The huge creamy-orange kitty with the rotund body and small head had lived about fourteen years, all but two of them with Miriam. The last few months of his life he was hobbling about on three legs because when he was younger, some cruel person had inflicted neurological damage to his shoulder muscles. I felt especially sorrowful about his death because when the doctor arrived, I'd picked kitty up from Dad's pillow where he was napping and brought him downstairs for his examination. TomTom had looked up sweetly into my face with complete peace and assurance in my ability to make him feel better. I felt that somehow I'd betrayed that trust to him as he struggled for his life and lost it on the kitchen floor.

As a believer in the afterlife for animal souls too, I decided to try something. I mentally communicated with TomTom to show me a sign by the end of May that he forgave me for what had transpired that dreadful day in the kitchen. Lest anyone think I'm completely off the wall, perhaps I can be forgiven because I was quite traumatized that month. We nearly lost Stripes to a blocked bladder in the beginning of May and Snuggles died nine days after TomTom. It was not a good month for pets.

One of my America Online Graphics friends sent me a link to a Message Board two weeks later after TomTom's passing. I hadn't browsed the board long before I came across the name of one of the posters. I couldn't believe what I saw and I rubbed my eyes. There was the name TomTom, spelled exactly the same way as my late feline friend!

As a postscript to this little tale, one other time I asked the poor old fellow for a sign that he was OK in Kitty Heaven. I nearly forgot the request until I turned on VH1 Oldies on Direct TV that night. Various videos from the 80's were playing. Suddenly one from the musical group The TomTom Club flashed on the screen. That was enough for me!

After feeling more comfortable on the Web, I decided that I needed to learn the basics of web page creation and make my own website. With the aid of some tutorials and some very helpful friends I created several sites including one I titled "My Memories of Mike," dedicated to you-know-who. Although not many people had visited it, those who had were gracious and kind in their compliments on the site.

What happened next was *really* odd. Once again, while waiting for a 3D picture of mine to render a sudden thought seemed to pop into my head. As you might recall from the "Chuzzlewit Episode" these ideas often come to me when I am in a rather meditative, almost hypnotic state. I pondered how interesting it would be if, against astronomical odds, a person should email me with the exact same name as Michael. In other words, another person named Michael William Hardesty. The reader is probably way ahead of me on this one. Yes, the next day I opened my email and someone who had visited the Mike Memorial site had written. His name was William Michael Hardesty! He had come across the web pages in his serendipitous search on the genealogy of the Hardesty family. The name was exactly the same only the order was reversed.

Over the years the number of unusual circumstances that I've come across while visiting the Web could fill a book by themselves. I shall end this chapter with a nod to a more spiritual happening. My grandma on Mom's side had always loved the old hymn "In the Garden." When Mom was alive I played it frequently on the Yamaha keyboard in her room using a slow gospel beat and a church organ or chorus voice. It seems that Michael's granny Mabel called that hymn one of her favorites as well.

One evening I was talking on the phone to Tom who, as I mentioned previously, had become a good friend of our family after Mike and Miriam died. He said he often found himself humming "In the Garden" without realizing it and he took that as a gesture from Mabel that she was keeping a loving and watchful eye on him. I thought so too. Part of the stanza in the song goes: "and He walks with me and He talks with me and He tells me I am His Own."

The next day after our phone conversation I checked my email. I had received a joke from a Florida friend of mine, which on its own accord is not noteworthy. But this ha-ha was about

Forrest Gump meeting St. Peter at the Pearly Gates. The punch line of the joke is the part where Forrest tells the Guardian "Shucks, St. Peter, that is the easiest [answer] of all. When I was a little boy, we sang a song in Sunday school and my mother sang it all the time about God; *ANDY WALKS WITH ME, ANDY TALKS WITH ME, ANDY TELLS ME I AM HIS OWN.*"

Chapter Thirteen

That Personal Touch

When the souls first pass on, I believe they have as much need to contact us as we have the need to hear from them. They miss us and want to reassure us that they're doing OK, not to worry. But they like to know that this message is getting across and we need to convey that to them. Those of us left behind in this world are not the only ones who seek encouragement. Our loved ones are eager to tell us that they have moved to a much better neighborhood. The real mystery is: what is their new "forwarding address?" Whatever agonies their minds and bodies might have endured on earth are cast aside the same way a caterpillar sheds its cocoon to become a dazzling butterfly.

Since they are no longer bound to a physical body, I think their full inborn "psychic" abilities come to the forefront, the same faculties that reside in us also, to a lesser degree. Whatever qualities the person has developed on the worldly plane follow him or her when they cross the threshold. In this world we are so caught up in everyday tasks that we don't have the time or the focus to concentrate on honing our intuitive communication skills. We rely on electronic devices to touch base with our friends and families. As long as we have an ample supply of AA batteries or a handy AC/DC outlet then we can get our messages across. Those fortunate individuals who can find a little time to sit in a quiet place to meditate daily are usually rewarded by heightened telepathic abilities.

On the Other Side, interaction appears to be pure telepathy, mind to mind thought transference. Money, so important on earth that people will kill for it, means nothing over there. Sex, drinking, smoking, gambling, drugs and other cravings eventually lose their hold on the souls who have crossed over and these are replaced with kindness, empathy, cooperation and love. Those souls who haven't been able to let go of earthly pleasures might not be terribly happy on the other side as long as they crave these indulgences more than the peace and spirituality that permeate the other realm. Some souls might become so earthbound that they are unwilling to venture forward in the afterlife at all and yet they are unable to go back to earth. Sometimes they may not even realize they are "dead" for many years! I think these souls are the "ghosts" that people perceive when they visit "haunted" houses.

That brings up another interesting observation. Throughout recorded history numerous people all over the globe have reported "deathbed visions" in which the loved one appears to them either in a very solid form, dressed in the same attire they normally wore or as a semi-transparent figure. Sometimes the observer merely sees a dark, smoky shape, vaguely human in outline. (My sister and I have seen a number of these rather scary "shades" over the years, only to discover within days that someone we know has passed!)

These visions invariably occur near the time of the loved one's death and that is verified later, but the observer had no way of *knowing* at the time of the vision that a person was dying. So many of these cases have occurred that the truth of this phenomenon seems beyond question. Often the newly departed soul even speaks to the astonished friend or family member. Recently crossed-over animal souls have been reported appearing the same way, and earthly animals will pick up something "strange" when a soul passes over. They will bark, meow, act restless or stare fixedly into space. Since most apparitions seem to occur when souls have just stepped over the portal or in the early months following death, is it possible that they still retain residual energy from the earth plane and thus are able to appear more dramatically before our "earthly" eyes? In one sense it is during this transitional period that they will miss our world the most since they have had little time to adjust to the beauty of the Other Side. Perhaps you might say they are a bit homesick.

There is an agreement among most students of the metaphysical that time is irrelevant in the other realm. I believe this concept to be true, yet I find it extremely hard to grasp this idea since I am very much a "clock watcher" here. Five years on earth might pass as five days over there. Because of this "time difference" (talk about *jet lag!*) it's possible that a departed soul will appear to those left on the earth plane much later than the aforementioned deathbed visions.

My personal theory on apparitions is that solid-looking phantasms are *more* likely to occur in souls who have passed over peacefully and naturally. There are of course no hard and fast rules on matters concerning the afterlife. Those who have died violently through accidents, murder or by their own hand might be so traumatized initially that their energy level is depleted and they don't have enough "oomph" to come across as a fully-realized materialization. But that does *not* mean that they are not communicating with us in other ways! My experiences with Michael have convinced me that he is very active mentally, exactly as he was when he lived right here in Virginia.

I didn't see Michael on Sunday, September 13, 1998, but as I lay down to take my afternoon nap, I felt his powerful presence. It was almost like the day when I had sensed him at Long Branch Nature Center. Only this time instead of perceiving that he was sad, I picked up that he was a warm and protective presence. I tried to shrug the whole thing off, thinking that my imagination was getting out of hand. "Wishful thinking," I muttered sleepily. But the feeling only grew stronger.

I finally spoke out loud to him, "Mike, if you really are here, please give me a sign, babe. I think I feel you near." I felt ridiculous. The phone rang downstairs at that moment but I felt too drowsy to get up and respond to it. The answering machine came on and I forced myself out of bed to hear what it was chattering about. I heard a lady's voice and she said she was from *The Washington Post.* She was calling to let me know my memorial notice for Michael was ready for publishing on October 10th and that he looked so good in his photo! I was quite astounded that she would call me on that particular afternoon since it was not even a business day but I guess Mike got his point across. An incident like that one persuaded me that my own intuition was good radar for detecting Mike.

Sudden odors, such as from a cigarette, after shave, perfume, floral scents or the sweet spicy odor of baking apple pie will often signal that a departed soul is hovering about. In Michael's case I will occasionally smell the unmistakable scent of Dial soap. He used to bathe with that brand and even washed his hair with it. Sandalwood incense will waft around the room at other times and yet nobody is burning any. Michael loved sandalwood and burned it in the bookstore all the time. These olfactory phantoms are like exquisite little grace notes in the musical scores of our lives. They add a nice touch to an otherwise dreary day and our departed loved ones know that. It's only polite to thank them for the wee gift they bring to us.

I think that our departed ones continue to take a very personal interest in us. They show us that they remember anniversaries, birthdays, weddings, holidays and other special days in most imaginative ways. In the case of Michael and me, our "anniversary" was always on the 28th of the month, since the December 28th Christmas party is when we first hooked up. Michael had made a card for me on our three-month anniversary, which was March 28, 1997.

He delighted in creating unique "homegrown" greeting cards, which usually consisted of a store-bought card that he embellished with various cutouts from magazines or newspapers. After he clipped the material, he would rubber cement it on the card, collage style. On this particular greeting he had pasted a rather interesting older couple inside and had captioned it, "MIKE and ROSY after 25 years. Still got a lot of that old Pazazz!" (He wasn't the world's greatest speller.) It always brought a smile to my face. I was cleaning out my dresser drawers and was rummaging through my old Mike cards on October 27, 1998 and I chuckled once more over that "Pazazz" one. On a whim I mentally asked Michael for an indication that he was still around, keeping an eye on things. I decided to ask him to send me another picture of the elderly couple within the next week. I had absolutely no idea who those people were and I thought it extremely unlikely I would ever run across a photograph of the distinctive duo again.

The very next evening, on the 28th, I was reading *The Washington Post* newspaper. I got to the Style section and my heart nearly jumped into my throat.

On the front page of that section was a photo of the old couple! It wasn't the exact same photo Michael had pasted on the card but I could certainly recognize the pair. By reading the accompanying article I learned that the lady was noted British author Iris Murdoch and the gentleman was her husband John Bayley. Either my precognitive abilities were getting very strong or Michael was sending me another "anniversary" gift. I prefer to believe the latter.

At times I think our dear departed ones are even capable of influencing animals and insects to convey messages of comfort to us. How many times after the death of a loved one have you heard of a graceful butterfly appearing out of nowhere and fluttering about the bereaved in an aerial ballet of sweetness and beauty? Often the beautiful insect will even land on the person's hand or head. These visitations frequently happen when the sorrowful one is feeling his or her most despondent. I recall a scene from the movie *Patch Adams* when Dr. Adams is teetering on the very edge of a precipice, feeling so alone in the world because his lady friend has recently died. When he wants a sign from his lost beloved that she still loves him and still exists, a gorgeous tiny butterfly appears and suddenly his spirits are lifted, as if on wings!

As a whole, I felt that I was coping with Michael's death

CHAPTER THIRTEEN

as well as could be expected and certainly the many confirmations that I believed he had sent me over the years were a great boost to my recovery. I bless him for taking the time and I hope to repay *him* someday for all the kindness he has shown me in the afterlife. His suicide may have traumatized people who loved him but I think he's been making amends for it. I wouldn't be at all surprised to learn that other folks who knew Michael have been experiencing "odd" things these past many years as well. I know I'm not the only one. Tom and Marion had some interesting experiences as has Mike's older daughter Robin and his grand-daughter Samantha.

Still, there are times when a poignant mood will take over. Such a night was September 30, 1999. The weather was clear and a bit chilly, as early fall often is in Virginia, and a huge, brilliant half moon hung over the horizon. A glittering display of stars carpeted the dark sky. It was nearly midnight when Jo and I decided to take a walk up our street. She was getting cold so she turned around for home when we reached the end of our drive. I continued on, ambling around the neighborhood, looking skyward. I cannot explain how lonely and empty I felt that autumn night. I heard the distant roar of traffic on Interstate 66 and I could see the orange-hued sodium vapor lights tinting the sky near the Metro station. Occasionally I heard a subway train squeal to a stop, start again and clickety-clack away into the darkness. I pondered how only two years earlier, the earth had contained an individual named Michael Hardesty and how one could merely travel a certain distance and reach this man. One could pick up the phone and hear his warm, comforting voice. But that evening he seemed as far away as the winking stars. Tears in my eyes, I pleaded silently with him to show me he still cared. I turned up a side road toward home. In the glare of a streetlight my eyes caught sight of a brown leaf lying squarely in the middle of the sidewalk some twenty feet in front of me. I expected the slight breeze to scatter it about and I anticipated the scratchy dry sound that it would make when it moved.

As I got closer I could see that is was no leaf at all but a little brown sparrow, looking pertly up at me, head cocked! What the wee bird was doing out at that hour of the night was anybody's guess. It was long past her bedtime. I became concerned that perhaps the creature was injured so I cautiously approached her. She continued to look at me with her bright eyes and with a tiny flute-like "tweet" she suddenly took flight and was gone in an instant. I was overcome with happy emotion.

Michael had had a thing for little brown sparrows. He once made a tape for me with a song titled "Little Brown Sparrow" by C.W. McCall included on the cassette. When he was a kid, he helped save a little brown sparrow from some mean boys who were trying to torture the tiny animal. And he loved Jo's lovely brown finch, Pee Wee. In fact, every time he visited our house, he insisted Pee Wee come out of her cage so she could perch on his finger! She was always happy to oblige. Extraordinary enough, certainly but there was more.

Later that week Tom Hardesty called from Iowa. We chatted about various subjects and I didn't mention the sparrow incident to him as I suspected he was growing a bit weary of my "Mikey sightings." Of his own accord he told me about a curious dream he had had a few nights earlier. Some of his dreams were quite amusing so I listened with interest.

In the dream, a little brown bird had appeared to him with some sort of important message from Mike. Tom said the bird seemed to be a sparrow of some sort. I gasped. Then I told him about *my* experience and he grew silent. I could tell it moved him very much. He asked me what night it had happened. As we compared notes, we realized that both the dream and the avian messenger had manifested the very same evening!

According to metaphysical books, erratic behavior involving electricity or electronics can sometimes indicate that a spirit is nearby. Television seemed to be the medium for a couple of odd experiences I had in connection with my dear friend. I should explain that at the time these two incidents occurred I rarely watched TV. We didn't receive the broadcast channels very clearly and only half a dozen came through in any case. That was before we subscribed to DirectTV satellite service with 150 plus channels. One evening I was tired but something told me to turn on the 11 o'clock news. It consisted of rehashed stories about Iraq but as I was on the point of turning it off, there was a segment about bounty hunters and I was idly thinking about one of Mike's friends who had this occupation. I no sooner got the thought out when who should appear on the screen but Mike's friend?

Another time I was up at seven in the morning, which is not characteristic for me. I am a night owl and going to *bed* at that time was more normal in my case. But that sunrise I was waiting for the local veterinarian's office to open so I could transport Stripes there. He had become deathly ill overnight with a blocked bladder and we had taken him to the emergency vet in Vienna for insertion of a catheter. Thank God he had stabilized, but he needed medication and observation at our regular vet office and we wanted to get an early start. I switched on the TV set to watch the early morning news. My ears perked up when they featured a story about a local crime that had been long unsolved. When they showed the detective assigned to that old case on the screen, I was shocked to see that is was the same fellow who been in charge of Michael's case! It was very bizarre since I never watched that particular morning show and unless Stripes had been ill and needed to be taken to the doctor, there is *no way* I would have seen that segment.

One thing about the afterlife that seems wonderfully comforting to me is how our loved ones seem to know when we need them the most. They are truly like our guardian angels, helping us climb the rugged mountains of life. The strongest evidence I had of this was when Mom had to be rushed to the hospital days before Thanksgiving 2001. I don't want to get into explicit medical details but suffice it to say that her symptoms indicated a severe bowel obstruction. She had been vomiting all day and her abdomen was horribly distended. The ambulance whisked her down to the medical center while Jo and I followed in our car.

We arrived at three in the afternoon and we sat in the waiting room for four hours until I was called back to the Emergency Room to see my mother. Because the ward was crowded with patients, the staff had put Mom in a bed located back in a small anteroom. There was another patient in the room too, next to Mom. He was a distinguished looking older gentleman who seemed to be fighting for breath.

I used to tell Michael how much I wished that life had a "Fast Forward" button so one could quickly bypass the unpleasant parts and yet could "Rewind" back to happier times. He wisely pointed out that by pushing the Fast Forward one assumed that the future was going to be better than the present, which wasn't necessarily so. All very true but I wanted the time to pass so I could discuss Mom's case with a doctor and go home. She looked so pale and ill in her bed. I was very worried and had not eaten anything all day, had just sipped a Coke. I'd developed a throbbing migraine and had ridden the crests of so many anxiety attacks that endless day that when seven o'clock rolled around, I was both physically and mentally exhausted. I felt like crying I was so miserable.

The son of the aforementioned patient in the bed next to my mother visited him, along with his wife. They were a most gracious couple and after the ice was broken, we three talked about many things including how difficult it was to care for one's incapacitated parents at home. In the next three hours the conversation somehow drifted to the subject of Germany. The son had grown up there in a military family and I commented how several months earlier, I had finished a pen and ink drawing of German philosopher Arthur Schopenhauer. I said that the drawing was meant for my boyfriend but that he'd never gotten to see it. The man wondered why he had not and I said my dear friend had ended his life prematurely. He sympathized.

Urged by some inner prompting, I then mentioned that my late friend had owned an antiquarian bookstore in the Bailey's

Crossroads area. In an instant he cried, "You must mean Mike! I bought books from his shop for years and so did my Dad and Mom. Mike could always find any book you wanted. He could talk about any subject under the sun!"

I was flabbergasted. What were the odds of my Mom being placed next to this gentleman and his family in such a large hospital? What were the chances that both our parents would take ill at the exact same time? As we talked further I realized that the son and his lovely wife actually knew Michael very well. They had enjoyed paying visits to the bookshop for a long time, and we had a wonderful chat about him before they left around ten o'clock.

My headache had subsided considerably and I felt much better. Before long I talked to the doctor who said Mom would be admitted to the hospital for a few days to be tested. I could go home.

She was released several days later, diagnosed with severe constipation and a stomach ulcer. She improved rapidly with medication. I said a long, thankful prayer to Michael for his support that Thanksgiving.

Chapter Fourteen

Melancholy Musings

The years rolled on and afterlife contact with Michael became an integral part of my life. I still thought of him as my friend, someone I continued to love with all my heart. Because I felt this way about him, I always tried to show appreciation for him in any way I could. I created a website for him, posted memorial notices annually in the paper, shared my photos of him, spoke of him to my friends, included him in many of my art projects and finally decided to write this book and publish it on Amazon.

I'm not a trained writer but I feel a powerful need to reach out to other people who might be experiencing the agony of depression and its deadly aftermath in their lives. **There is a chance that this book might touch one person's life, might help someone through a dark night, just as the souls in the afterlife seem to flock to our aid when we cry out to them.** I think Michael would want me to write this book; I hope so at least.

A clinical discussion of depression is beyond my expertise and outside the scope of this book. But depression *can* be treated with proper medications and therapy and most of all, with a supportive, loving network of friends and family. Half the battle in conquering it is *realizing what it is and realizing that you are not alone.* Millions of people suffer from this affliction and there is absolutely no shame in it. *It is not your fault.* Guilt seems to be intricately interwoven in the fabric of melancholy but it only causes the other symptoms to loom larger than they really are. There are many excellent books about this dreaded disorder, including one I mentioned earlier, *Darkness Visible* by

William Styron. The disease can mimic numerous other conditions and that is one reason that it is so insidious. It sneaks up on a person when he or she least expects it.

Michael's depression first manifested itself as an inability to sleep well. He found it hard to fall off and remain in slumber. He tried natural herbal remedies such as valerian root, chamomile, St. John's Wort, tryptophan tablets, and the more traditional therapies like warm milk and soothing baths. Finally he was put on Ativan and later Ambien but still sweet dreams eluded him. The less sleep he got the more worried and anxious he became. Soon he was barely dragging through his day. Fixing TV sets and dealing with his customers became exhausting. The color was bleaching out of his life.

Ironically, some depressed people sleep way too much. They can barely get out of bed they feel so tired and low. Various aches and pains afflict the body, causing the person to wonder whether they might not have a serious disease like cancer. In Michael's case, his back and his heart especially bothered him. Anxiety and panic attacks began to appear, often seemingly out of the blue. His heart would race and his thoughts would run in an endless circle, like a dog chasing its tail. He would become nauseated, pale and very agitated. At such times, he was sure death was imminent. He would sweat profusely during the attacks, something he had never done when he was healthy. As a consequence of these episodes, he became afraid to venture out in locations where he had experienced panic and the areas where he felt safe and comfortable diminished daily.

Having lived through innumerable anxiety situations myself, I found it painful to see Michael this way and I tried to be brave, but inside, my own distress was spiraling out of control. No matter what I did, it never seemed to really get to the root of the problem. *I have never felt so helpless.* If I had to do it again, I would have insisted on joint counseling for Michael and me. He had considered seeing a local psychiatrist who didn't believe in the use of drugs to treat depression, but much as I regret it now, I was lukewarm about the idea at the time. It's not that I discouraged him with this but I didn't exactly act as a cheerleader either.

The worst part of the despondency was how it caused Michael to perceive himself. He began to feel like a shadow of his former self, an invalid and only half a man. For someone who had always been young at heart, feeling suddenly old was catastrophic for him. Despite knowing deep inside that he was a good person, he also felt guilty as if he had done something horribly wrong.

He became paranoid, seeing ominous signs in ordinary things. For example, he thought a flock of crows in his backyard was after him or Squeeky before she died. He had fears that the crows would seize her and would carry the little cat away, like those winged monkeys did with the characters on *The Wizard of Oz*. Another time he suspected he might actually have "mad cow disease."

I believe it is this aspect of depression that attacks the self-esteem, the relentless chipping away of the personality that leads to the final act, suicide. The depressed person must be made to still feel worthy, to feel loved. They should not be chastised for something they have no control over. They may have become dependent and childish in many ways, but they cannot control this. More than anything in the world the person wants to feel better, to be well again. They yearn for their independence and joie de vivre again. Most hate to be a burden to those they love and I suspect the prospect of such a thing is very threatening in their tortured minds.

When Mike attempted suicide the first time it was a little over three weeks before his actual death. The day before this attempt he had been acting peculiarly. Marion reported to me that Michael had told her that he thought he would have to "let me go." He planned to call and break it off with me! I was stunned and miserable and didn't understand this, since we had seen each only other a few days earlier and had gotten along fine when Jo and I had visited the bookstore. When he called me from work that afternoon I was upset. He never got around to handing me a "Dear Joan" letter because Marion had forewarned me about the situation.

"Hi Rosy. How are things?"

"Not so good."

"What's up?"

"Why don't you tell *me* what's up, Mike? I've heard some strange things. If you want me out of your life just spill it! But I think you are making a serious mistake. Many people go their whole life and never find the affinity we have and now you want to just flush it all down the toilet? It's like you're blaming me for your depression! Do you want to go back to that old girlfriend?" I asked in reference to a relationship he had been in prior to meeting me.

"No, I doubt that it would work out with her. But I have to think of all possibilities Rosy. At this point I'm just grasping at straws trying to understand this thing. Maybe we should put our relationship on a back burner for awhile?"

"Fine. I can understand that, I can deal with that. I'm here for you. But don't just throw it all away! Please don't make a judgment like that while you're not feeling well."

After our conversation, he called Marion again and told her he thought he would be making the biggest mistake imaginable to push me out of his life. He called back and apologized.

"I don't know what I was thinking, Pudder. I'm sorry but I need to try to get at the root of this damned male menopause or whatever it is! I know you love me and have been behind me every step of the way. Every step and I appreciate it."

I was sobbing on the other end, but I could comprehend on some level that he might place blame on me for his feeling bad since it seemed to happen after I had come into his life. But the thought made me feel horrible, like some kind of monster! I began to wonder if my anxiety attacks had somehow triggered the whole disorder or I had inadvertently said or done something wrong to start this mental avalanche in his life. I began to believe that I might have a curse on me. The depression and guilt he was feeling were reaching me too, as if through mental osmosis. Life was fast turning into a miserable nightmare for both of us.

He called me again around eleven o'clock that night and mentioned that he wanted to sleep and planned to take an extra Ambien or two. I warned him not to take more than the prescribed dose of any of his medications but he reassured me he would be fine. He had a Mid-western stubborn streak that could be hard to deal with at times. Mike was certainly an independent man. But the thought of his taking too many pills worried me so much that I drove out to his house a half-hour later. There was a full September moon that night which had broken through the clouds after an earlier thunderstorm. Retreating storm clouds still clung to the eastern horizon, occasionally flickering with bright orange lightning. When I reached his house, all was pitch black and silent. I debated whether I should ring his bell or just leave him be. I knew how hard it was for him to sleep and the last thing I wanted to do was to interrupt his slumber if he had managed to doze off. On the other hand, could I really trust him with those pills? The dilemma was tying me up in knots. Finally I decided to leave without letting him know I was there, but I said a fervent prayer for his protection nonetheless.

As I drove home along lonely, wandering Prosperity Avenue I screeched to a halt. There in the middle of the road was a huge, black gnarled tree branch, blocking the pavement on one side! It resembled an enormous evil snake in shape. I guess the storm had knocked it down an hour or so earlier. I reversed and carefully went around the fallen branch. The silvery shimmer of moonlight on the road put me in a melancholy mood. As someone who had more than a passing knowledge of astrology, I knew that a full moon in September was usually in the sign of Pisces, when the sun was in Virgo. Such a moon was called a "suicide moon" in the old days because more people statistically died by their own hand when that configuration occurred. I was in a morbid mood that night.

Later, the phone rang at three o'clock in the morning and it was Mike. "Hello, is this my night nurse?" he joked weakly. "I have those two little stuffed bears you bought me here and I'm looking at them beside my bed, Mikey Bear, in his sailor outfit and Rosy Bear in her pretty dress. They look so cute together!" He sounded like he was crying.

"Hi Mike. Are you OK? You sound so sad! What are your plush bears doing there? I thought you normally kept them on that shelf at the shop!"

"I brought them home so I could look at them and feel better. I have my Hawaiian shirt that I wore on our fun trip to Manassas hanging up too, so I can remember that wonderful day we had last Fourth of July. We were so happy, weren't we Pee Wee? That was the best day of my life. I mean it."

"Mine too, but we'll be happy again. You'll see, honey. We'll go to lots of other small towns and have a great time! When the leaves change it will be beautiful. Halloween is your favorite holiday, isn't it? That's coming up before you know it! And think of Christmas in the snow." I said, sniffling and dabbing at my eyes with a tissue.

"Yes I love Halloween. We will have fun again, won't we? Rosy...no matter what happens, I just want you to know I'll always be there for you. Always. You just call on me and I'll be around. And somehow, some way, some day, we'll be together again. I promise you that. I'll find a way. You know because we're like Romeo and Juliet. Rosy, they just won't let us be, will they?" he said cryptically. "Our families, I mean," he added. "Like the Capulets and Montagues."

"Well my Dad can be a pain in the ass at times." I didn't really understand what he had meant by "families" but it must have worried him. I was sobbing at that point, gravely concerned about his frame of mind, and I was trying to think of hopeful, positive things to tell him. "I'm making my special home-made vegetable beef soup tonight, Mike. Smells so good! Wish you were here to have some. Yummy." I slurped over the phone.

He laughed a little. Then I confessed that I had spied on his house earlier that night.

"Why didn't you stop by to see me?" he said.

"I was afraid you were asleep and I didn't want to wake you."

"I slept for a couple hours actually. Rosy I'm going to try to get more sleep but I just wanted to call and talk to you. Will you be up awhile in case I want to call again?"

"Sure, making soup and thinking about you, boy."

"I love you and I'll think of happier times, dream of happier times, OK?"

"OK. You do that and so will I, Mike. Sleep well and know how special you are to me! Love you. Good-bye."

Five hours later he called 9-11 in desperation, pistol to his head and they took him to Mount Vernon Hospital. After four days he released himself. He told me later that he had left suicide notes all over the house that dreadful morning.

The last time I ever saw Michael at work was Wednesday, October 1st. When he came out of the hospital, he seemed somewhat rejuvenated and he tried to focus on doing things to improve his business. He decided to cut one of his two business phone lines and eliminate the two Yellow Page ads advertising Mike's Antiques and Mike's Records. He still retained Mike's TV and Mike's Books but I felt a pang of sympathy when he removed the antiques and records because I could recall vividly how happy and proud he had been in early 1997 when the ads came out in the books. Nearly every day he would ask me, "Did you get your Yellow Pages yet? Go check out my ads! All four of em! They look real swell, don't they?" he said, excited as a kid about them. He also wanted to re-hang his draperies in the front shop window and I bought some curtain hardware for him to do that. Things were shaping up.

He commissioned me to paint two large wooden signs for him, one with Rodin's "The Thinker" featured on it to advertise his book business. I made that one quite fancy with Old English black and red lettering and a gilt border. The other sign was for "Mike's TV Repair," a more straightforward black and red placard that he intended to prop up against his station wagon in the parking lot so drivers passing on Columbia Pike could see it and stop. This was the one I was working on when I last saw him. I had toted it into his shop that Wednesday afternoon along with some mineral spirits, lettering brushes and small cans of red and black glossy paint. I had partially finished the sign, penciling in all the letters and leaving some unpainted so he could fill them in himself. He enjoyed painting and he thought it would be fun to swing the brushes again. When he saw me come in the door, he walked up and gave me a warm hug and a broad grin, just like always. I noted that he looked rather thin and tired however. Then he said, "Guess who called today?"

"Who?"

"Dr. B, that guy who has the office in Maryland. I had called him earlier today. We discussed my case a little but I can't afford his fees. Oh well, I think I'm getting better on my own."

If I had been thinking clearly back then, I would have taken the cue, would have said, "Well good! Don't worry about the fee, I'll cover it. The important thing is that you believe in this guy and his treatment. We'll go there as soon as we can. I'll drive you if you want!"

In my fantasies I always wonder what would have happened if I had done that. After Michael's death I read this person's book and was so impressed with what he espoused that I felt deep regret that I had not been more supportive of his work. This psychiatrist in all his years of practice **had never lost a single person to suicide.** But I didn't know such things on that October day so I merely said, "Darn. I'm sorry Mike. But you *are* getting better, I can tell!"

Then he hoisted the sign up on the workbench and began to letter with the strongly pungent oil paints.

"Rosy, why don't you run to Safeway and get us something to eat for lunch."

"OK what do you want?"

"Hmm. I don't know, maybe some kind of meat thing and maybe some fruit and those strawberry milk drinks that folks use for nutrition. You know, like Ensure. Charles (Miriam's husband) talked to me on the phone a little while ago and he said they're really good. Meanwhile I'll try and finish the sign." He handed me twenty dollars.

"That looks really nice," I noted as he filled in some of the letters with red paint. He had the radio turned to a rock station and had some of his old swagger back as he wielded the brush and grinned happily at me.

I spent about twenty minutes at the crowded store, which was only two blocks up the street from him.

As I got back into the car after purchasing things for lunch, I felt good. The air was still mild, the sun was shining and Michael was getting back on track. Months later I learned that he had written in his journal about attempting suicide a second time the previous night: a razor slash to his arm.

When I pulled my Honda into the parking lot of Mike's TV I was aghast! Three police cars, lights flashing were parked in my usual place. My heart leaped into my throat as sheer panic overtook me. People were milling about outside and I began to hyperventilate as I searched desperately for a free parking space on the nearby hill.

"Oh dear God no! Please no. Don't tell me he's killed himself in there while I was gone!" I moaned out loud. I was engulfed in pure, mind-gripping adrenaline as tears began to pour. **It was so unfair! Every time I started feeling better about Mike something dashed my hopes**. I grabbed the bag containing our lunch and got out of the car, legs shaky. My heart was pounding so hard as I approached the store that I nearly blacked out. A policeman blocked my way and the people outside were shouting in some foreign tongue.

"Ma'am I can't let you in here," the cop said.

"But I'm his girlfriend! I brought him lunch!" I babbled.

The police officer looked at me searchingly and was silent for several seconds. I must have appeared hysterical to him. Finally he said,

"Oh OK. Then you can go in. Sorry, didn't know."

I rushed in expecting the worse and was overcome with relief when I saw Mike standing against the workbench, brush in hand, talking to another police officer. He looked very pale and had his magnifier goggles pushed back from his hair, causing his hair to spike out in all directions.

He motioned me over. "Hi sweetie. Just put the food over there and I'll be with you in a minute," he said with a nervous smile.

After some time it became clear that the hubbub was merely a dispute with a disgruntled customer who had become rather unruly and someone had called the cops. When the officers left, Mike turned to me, and embraced me tightly. I could feel his body trembling and he had broken out in a sweat. "Oh God Rosy. I can't finish the sign. Please finish it for me? My hands are shaking so bad!" and indeed they were. He grabbed the bag from the store and popped the top on one of the strawberry drinks, finishing it in one long gulp. "These things don't taste so hot, despite what Charles said," he grimaced. He made a good-sized belch and we both chuckled.

I smoothed out his hair and told him, "It's OK baby. Just relax and enjoy your lunch. I'll finish this in no time, Mike." When I completed it, he came over to the bench and pronounced the sign a success as he set it aside to dry.

He was seated in his dilapidated, comfortable old swivel chair and I was perched on his diner stool. It was late afternoon by then and nearly closing time. By the illumination of the overhead fluorescent lights I noticed a laceration on his upper right forearm, about an inch and a half long. It looked like a cat scratch to me and because I knew he still owned Magic (Squeeky had died only days before) I didn't say anything.

He looked over at me, a scared, haunted, pleading look in his dark brown eyes. It broke my heart to see it. His eyes begged, "Rosy please help me. Please do something to make living worthwhile! I want to live so much but I'm fading away." But he remained silent.

"Mike you have the most beautiful eyes, honey. They're so

deep, soft and soulful." I squeezed his still shaky hands tightly.

"No Pudder, you have the beautiful eyes," he answered as he drew close. I sat on his lap a few minutes just holding him, stroking his silky Dial soap-scented hair and kissing him gently, like one does a child when he is not feeling well.

"Please come over to my house tonight?" he asked, looking up.

"Sure Mike. I'd love to," I answered. "But I better go now. It's getting late and I have to help Jo make dinner."

When I left the shop and started my car, I saw Mike walk up to the door, peering out the glass as he always did when I departed. He smiled sadly and gave me a parting wave. In my rear view mirror I could see his eyes following my car all the way out to Columbia Pike. I never guessed that Fate would arrange that to be my final visit to his little bookstore.

Later that night we had a quiet evening at his house and Michael seemed much better than he had earlier. It felt like old times. I didn't stay too long because I knew he had experienced a long, tiring day. We parted and I felt lighter in my heart.

The last time I ever saw Michael turned out to be thirty-two hours before he ended his life. It was a warm night for autumn, with a nearly full moon peeking out from ghostly clouds that scudded across the sky. At the shop that day Michael had set up his TV sign that we had painted the week earlier and it had attracted some new customers. Because of that he was encouraged enough to pass out some TV repair flyers, printed years earlier, to nearby apartment buildings.

He invited me over to his house, requesting me to please stop by Shopper's Food Warehouse on John Marr Drive in Annandale on my way over, to pick up some items for him. To this day I can recall those items and how much they cost, as if they are branded into my memory: Del Monte canned pears, Scott paper towels, Chock Full O'Nuts coffee, two Stouffers Salisbury Steak dinners and Dial soap. The total was $17.99. As I left the grocery store and walked across the parking lot to my car, I looked up at the moon and an involuntary shiver and whisper of melancholy went through my body. When I reached his door, he was shirtless and he greeted me with a huge bear hug, squeezing me so tightly I could barely breathe.

"Hey is that you Mike or a boa constrictor?" I joked

"I'm so glad to see you Rosy. I never want to let you go 'cause it feels so good to hold you. Thanks so much for the groceries, sweetie. How much do I owe you?" he said pulling his wallet from his shorts pocket. They looked like the same ones he had worn during our Independence Day jaunt at Manassas three months before.

"Nah, forget it!" I waved the money away. "It's on me."

"Why are you so good to me?"

"Because I love you, silly!"

He cracked a smile but looked very thin and quite unwell to me. Almost as soon as I put the groceries on the kitchen table he started heating up the Stouffers dinners in the microwave, both packages.

"I hope you're eating both of those Mike because I don't want any!" I exclaimed.

"I thought you were hungry. I thought both of us were going to sit down and have dinner," he said, looking puzzled. But even though it was past eight o'clock, I had no appetite. He put one dinner back in the freezer and devoured his dish in record speed.

"I have some nice chocolate swirl ice cream for us for dessert. Want a beer?"

I took the Schlitz from him and asked him if he was capable of drinking again, but he told me that his son-in-law had brought over the beverage and he had not drunk any. However he did take one tiny sip of mine. We went up to his room where he showed me a chart that he had made, chronicling his symptoms and medications over the past several months. It looked very thorough and it was apparent that he was very serious about solving the medical mystery that was tormenting his life. He intended to visit Woodburn or Kaiser Permanente the following day and wanted to present the medical log to the doctors in charge. I knew he kept a daily journal too, a large spiral bound notebook where he scribbled entries with whatever was handy, pen or stubby pencil.

"So Pose, what are we going to do?" he asked, pulling me close and reclining on his bed. "We've got to solve this thing, get to the bottom of it! I'm determined to be like Sherlock Holmes and unravel this mystery! Hey, I have an idea. How about I stay at your house for awhile, maybe in your basement? You think that would work?"

"Well," I said hesitantly, "I just don't know about that Mike. You know with my Dad and looking after my Mom and all." Secretly I was rather shocked he would even suggest such a thing, knowing my family situation but I surmised he must have felt desperate to have even asked it. I didn't think Jo would be happy with it either as she valued her privacy in our basement as she surfed the web and created art on her computer. But I was willing to try it and told him so.

"I have another idea. Here's the deal. Maybe both you and Monica could move in with me and take turns caring for me until I get back on my feet soon!"

"Now that just might work. Mike I'm perfectly willing," I replied thinking it sounded like a more sensible idea than his moving into my house. "We'd have to clear out your second bathroom though, no more storing books and magazines in there! When you have two ladies in the house you need two working bathrooms!" I joked.

He laughed. "No problem."

We daydreamed about how wonderful it would be to leave the city and buy a little antique bookstore out in the country, living over the establishment.

We began to watch TV and suddenly he made a request. "Could you please go downstairs to the dryer and bring up my clothes? I just heard the buzzer go off."

I complied and brought in an armful of warm, clean smelling laundry. I folded the towels and put them in the linen closet and put his shirts and jeans into his big wooden dresser. At his urging I hung his new tee shirt that Jo had given him for his birthday on a hanger attached to his sunlamp. It was a light gray color and had a timber wolf silk-screened on the front of it.

"I want to wear that to work tomorrow," he said. Then he had an unusual request.

"Please give me that light blue flannel pajama top Rosy. I want to wear it and feel the warmth from the dryer on my chest. I want to picture how happy we will be when you, Monica and me will live here. I'll be back to my old self in no time with your care!"

He pulled me close and said, "Listen to my heart. Does it sound good to you?"

"Sure does," I replied my head resting on his chest listening to the rhythmic drumbeat of life. Yet, I was concerned about him. Michael looked terribly gaunt and had dark circles under his eyes. His hair had grown out and was shaggy around his neck. His legs seemed to have a fine tremor in them. In some peculiar way, this slender appearance made him look younger, boyish even but in a gamin-like way. Even though I loved being close to him like that, a growing uneasiness was filling my mind. As we lay there, just enjoying each other's company, I grabbed his right hand and began to caress it, squeezing it and interlocking our fingers, over and over. A large lunar moth was flying around the room and suddenly it landed on his cheek.

"Hey you got a bug on your face!" I joked and I reached over to brush it away.

But he just intercepted my hand and told me, "Let him stay there."

When I turned to look at him he had a very strange expression on his face, one I had never seen before. He was looking directly into my eyes and he looked very serious, deeply sad and earnest but at the same time he also looked detached. It was a paradoxical expression somehow both warm and cool and it gave me goose bumps. I turned back around and my eyes lighted on his open closet door. I knew he had cleaned the closet out very recently.

In the glow of his bedside lamp I could see clothes hanging

up but peeking out from behind one of his shirts I saw something else: a bullet belt with one shell in particular shining a golden color in the lamp light. I shuddered and looked back at him. His eyes went from my face toward the closet and fear clutched at my heart.

In hindsight, why I didn't mention the bullet belt at that moment and demand to know if Michael was hiding guns in the house is beyond me. After all, if he truly possessed no guns, why would he still have ammunition around? Perhaps I was afraid of his answer, perhaps I was in denial, and maybe I was just plain stupid. But that is how it happened, our macabre last dance together holding each other and denying all the hell that was happening around us. We could enjoy one final time together. But the clock was striking midnight...

I left for home that long ago evening, feeling Mike's love like a balm as I waved goodbye to him standing on his front porch, still wearing the blue flannel pajama top and shorts. The setting moon lit up the scene as we bade farewell.

We talked on the phone the next day at least six different times, making plans for a future that was already past. But we never saw each other again.

Mike used to say he thought people committed suicide because they saw situations in their lives as a long, downward spiral. Their life might not appear so bad to other people but to them, they could see no way but down and that they anticipated things getting even worse. It was the fear of *further* loss that drove them to the final desperate act.

People die by their own hand for many different reasons of course, but I am struck by how many people who have chosen that route are actually rare, caring individuals. Under normal circumstances, they would never dream of hurting anyone and yet that is exactly what their death does, in spades. Their final heartrending act seems selfish but the rest of their lives speak volumes to the contrary. Those who knew the departed one will often remark on how kind, sweet, helpful, remarkable and special their loved one was. Their unique personalities were like beacons shining in this dark world and their passing made the earth a dimmer place. This planet can ill-afford to lose such souls. But then perhaps we never do lose them…

Chapter Fifteen

The Decision

Two and a half years had passed since that Black Friday in October 1997. An idea gradually began to form in my mind. I felt that Michael was still around me and remained my friend but somehow I wanted an "official seal of approval" on my experiences, a third party confirmation. I also wanted more insight into exactly why he had ended his life that tragic morning. Many puzzle pieces remained missing.

I thought of Mr. George Anderson, who is a world renowned psychic medium with years of experience in communicating with those souls we call "dead."

I knew that inquisitive scientists had tested George on numerous occasions, wiring him with electrodes, examining him for telepathy, and attempting to disclaim his powers. Despite all this, Mr. Anderson had calmly and steadfastly continued to relay otherworldly messages he received to grieving people, and he somehow had managed to retain a sense of humor about the whole thing. What impressed me is that he never seemed intimidated by all the probing. He had acquired his "gift" as a small child after a bout with a serious illness, and he had braved ridicule and heartache for expressing his unusual powers during most of his youth. The books chronicling Mr. Anderson's gift lifted my heart and I decided to take the plunge. I was going to schedule a "discernment" with him! But first I had to square it away with Michael.

Perhaps it was the nostalgic hint of spring in the air but my resolve to obtain a reading became crystallized in March 2000. I decided to ask Mr. Hardesty once again (so what else is new?)

for signs that he wanted the reading too. I wasn't going to make things too easy because I was determined that if my idea was valid, then the signs would appear. I needed to think I had Michael's approval since the waiting list for Mr. Anderson's discernments was long and the readings were not inexpensive.

On George Anderson's website, I noticed that the next available telephone appointment was for August 10th that year. I wouldn't be able to travel to New York so a phone session seemed to be the only way to go. Thus, my first sign to be on the lookout for was to see the date *"August 10th"* somewhere by the end of March. Perhaps not the most logical way of going about verification but the best I could do in the circumstances.

Sign number two. I needed the money for the reading. Somehow, some way, funds would have to come my way by March 31st. This was a toughie. I have never received money out of the blue in my entire life.

Sign number three and the final sign would be for me to see something about George Anderson in the media by March's final day.

Needless to say, all three events had transpired by month's end! I was jubilant and wrote to Mr. Anderson's organization to schedule a reading with him.

In a nutshell, here is how the signs panned out:

1. I was watching a British-produced video rented from the Mary Riley Styles Library. (I find it curious how that particular library seemed to play an important role in several "psychic events" related to Mike.) The series was about bomb squads detonating unexploded munitions after World War 2. I wasn't even thinking about the George Anderson reading at the time but suddenly on the TV screen I saw a vintage desk calendar and boldly dispayed on its page was the date "August 10th." One down and two to go!

2. My father's twin brother Jervas had died tragically as the result of an electrical fire in his mobile home in May 1999. Dad was quite distraught since the boys had been close most of their

lives. Jervas had lived in the trailer since his retirement in the mid-seventies as staff photographer for the *Des Moines Register and Tribune.* He didn't have much in the way of earthly goods except his heirloom cameras and old vintage movie reels and sadly, they had been destroyed in the blaze. But apparently Jervas had $6,000 in his credit union, which he willed to their younger sister Pat. Aunt Pat had always been a gracious soul and to our complete astonishment she very kindly forwarded the money to our family! That is the check I mentioned earlier in this story that Michael seemed to be "worried" about, the one I suspect he concealed away behind our French table clock.

3. Finally, by month's end I saw Mr. George Anderson on a primetime TV special.

I received notification of my upcoming George meeting in May. I was ecstatic! The discerment was scheduled for March 15, 2001, 6:00 P.M. In the meanwhile, I needed to get things prepared. I knew I wanted to tape the session so I bought a telephone-answering device for recording long messages. To be doubly sure I would get the best quality recording, I also rigged up my boom box with a microphone and batteries in case of a power outage. March in Virginia is notorious for sending unforeseen, heavy wet snowstorms that blanket the power lines at inopportune times. I bought a full duplex speakerphone. I was going high tech and the reading was still months away.

To prepare for the reading, I re-read Mr. Anderson's books and tried to psyche myself mentally for what was to come. I was really excited and began to count down the days, until a paragraph in one of his books *stopped me cold in my tracks*. It explained that sometimes in a reading the very person one wants to connect with does *not* appear because the person being read gets too emotional, too anxious and the energy doesn't flow well. I hadn't thought of that but it made sense. I began to fret that maybe I would want Michael to communicate with me *so* much that I would keep him away with that very wish! Overtrying as it were.

But the months seem to simultaneously drag by and fly by. How is it possible? Before I knew it, my birthday had arrived at the end of February and March roared in the next day like a lion. Only two more weeks! To say I was getting the jitters was a serious understatement. Suppose I was making a huge mistake? Suppose Michael didn't really want to "talk" to me after all, despite all the signs he had appeared to send my way? Suppose he was angry with me for pestering him? Suppose there wasn't really such a thing as an afterlife anyhow; it was all a series of odds-defying coincidences? Suppose...

Finally the big day arrived. It was a gloomy, raw day with rain threatening. I awoke and sat up in bed. A small photo of Michael was on my night table and I talked to him, this time right out loud.

"Please Michael," I beseeched, "Come to the discernment today. I want that more than anything in God's universe. I mean it! Nothing would mean more to me. I know I can't tell you to come or force you to; you've got to come of your own free will. But baby, I miss you so terribly and I want to talk with you once again. Don't you want to talk to me too? And when you *do* show up, *please* try to get on the scene as soon as possible because I'm *so* nervous! Oh please don't let me down..." I wailed. I was pathetic, but that's what I did. Mike's photograph just stared back at me, enigmatically.

Jo and I took an afternoon walk and it began to rain in earnest. We silently plodded along the slippery sidewalks, wielding our umbrellas. I felt like I was scheduled to visit the electric chair in a few short hours. After we returned home, I made sure all my equipment was set up properly and I tested and retested the tape machines several times. It was a wonder the cassette tapes didn't stretch and break from all the experimenting. I was so jumpy by late afternoon that I could hardly stand it. I peered out the basement door and spied two fat mourning doves perched on the back fence, oblivious to the pouring rain and cooing to each other. How I envied those birds!

I was dressed up in a new Shepler's western shirt and boots

and wore one of Mike's old black cowboy hats on my head. After all, it *was* rather like a date, wasn't it? I brushed my hair to a silky blonde sheen. I had bought a large raspberry scented candle and I lit that, trying to calm my wildly beating heart as I glanced at my digital watch every minute or so. I was not afraid of "ghosts" or "spirits" or Mr. Anderson. He seemed like a nice fellow on TV and from the books but I was horribly afraid Michael would not show. Jo played music on her computer's Real Player jukebox as we tried to settle down for the zero hour.

I expected George to be prompt, as twenty-four hours earlier Mr. Andrew Barone, George Anderson's program director had called to verify the appointment today. Then, my watch showed six o'clock and still no phone call. I was trying to calm myself by staring into the candle flame and breathing deeply. I felt ill I was so tense.

A minute later the phone rang stridently. I jumped like a startled cat and picked the receiver up on the first ring, heart in my throat…

Chapter Sixteen

The Big Day

(Mr. Anderson's words in **boldface**)

Hello?
Hi, it's George calling.
Hi George, how are you doing?
Good. How are you?
Pretty good.
Good. Ok, before we begin, just a quick setup. Number one, whatever I say to you, just respond with "yes" or that you understand.
OK.
Also make sure that you do respond out loud not only so that your loved ones like to hear your voice but also we're on the phone.
Yes *(laughing a bit)*
I've got to hear that, you know that it's making sense to you.
OK.
And keep in mind, you know, other people may come to say "hello" and if you *do* recognize the name, don't say "no" because, you know, you weren't close, they died a long time ago or whatever. Just say "yes" so I can bring them through and they can say their thing. Also just don't help during the session. I mean don't ask about someone. Don't help me with names.
OK.
The souls have to do the work. And if they don't, I drop it then it's up to them to bring it back again or clarify it, but I just want them to...they have to prove themselves.

They sure do!
I'm very rigid about it.
OK.
I'm probably worse than anybody is when it comes to that. Well, there are so many people out there claiming they're doing it and they're not.
Yes. I know! *(Laughing nervously)*
And *(laughing a little)* **I don't want to sound conceited, but I say to myself, if this is really happening then they have to prove it and I know it's really happening. And if they can't prove it I know they can't work miracles and they won't do it the way *I* think they should do it...**
Right
But the thing is, I expect them to prove themselves. So, let's begin!
OK.
So without further delay we'll start and as I said just keep it "yes" or that you understand. And let's see...

Ok, well immediately a male presence has come forward. I'm sure you understand somehow.
Yes.
Actually another male and a female just came into the room as well. Now let me just be careful with this. A male presence comes near to you in a fatherly manner.
Uh...No.
Uh, no, no, no! He didn't say he was your dad! He just came in a fatherly manner. So I have to go with that because that could mean many different interpretations.
Uh huh.
But that's why I immediately said that this one didn't say he was your dad but he comes to you...
I see.
In a fatherly manner.
Yes.
Uh, also there's a younger male too, yes?

Yes.

Yeah 'cause somebody...Wait a minute...Looks like people stepping over each other.

(Laughing nervously and loudly)

The younger male pushed forward saying he was here first!

(Laughing)

So he should go first. Because this other male started coming forward in a fatherly manner who did declare, who does declare now that he is a grandfather. I'm sure one of your grandfathers has passed.

Yes. Both.

And I'm not going to be funny about it, I'm just going to say that he's announcing he's here and let's leave it at that for the moment because the younger male keeps pushing forward who is family he states. Yes?

No.

Well, can I say by choice then?

By choice?

Yeah, because I should have explained that to you in the beginning. When they come in as family, it's, you know, like my best friend is like one of the family?

Yes.

It's this sort of thing. He came in as family. When you said "no" he was like "What do you mean "*no*?" Then he said, well, by choice. "Term of endearment" family.

OK. Yes.

But he did pass young by the standard of the day, yes?

Yes.

Because he *does* put a big heart in front of you. You understand?

Yes.

Because he says he has great fondness for you. Understood?

Yes.

Because he's kind of laughing at you, like he puts the big heart in front of you, you acknowledge that "yes" he says "I have great fondness for you but I'm not worthy enough to be considered family?"

(Laughing)
He's kind of teasing you like…
(Laughing) Yeah, that…Yes.
"Your point is invalid so to speak" as he says. But… yeah 'cause he says you're his sweetheart.
Yes.
Yeah, 'cause that's what he states. That you and he share romantic attraction.
Yes.
And so…because he says you and he are one in the heart.
Yes.
So again he's laughing at you like "But I'm not your family?" You know again, by choice, yes.
I wish!
But the thing is, as he states you and he certainly shared romance and as he says "Marriage in the heart."
Yes.
And he just stated your hope…that you were very much hoping to hear from him.
Yes.
So that's why he says he kind of pushed your grandfather aside like "Hey I got here first and I'm the one she wants to hear from!"
Yes *(giggling)* Sounds like him.
But the thing is, he has…I like his personality. He comes across kind of like with a wacky sense of humor.
Oh yeah.
And a lot of fun and it is just apparent that as he says you complement that. So you and he apparently always got along very well.
Yes.
Because as he states "We were not only husband and wife so to speak, we were great friends."
Yes!
And that's the important part. You loved being in each other's company.

Yes.
And he says even though your heart's broken that he's passed on, he still is very much in your company.
Oh...
Spiritually.
That's good to hear!
Because as he says, he's around you like as a guardian angel so to speak, and you shouldn't be the least surprised to hear that!
Yes! Well no. I'm not surprised.
Yeah I know. I know what you meant. That's there.
He admits he didn't have the easiest life on the earth, true?
Yes.
He's not too disappointed to be away from here.
Yes.
Away from the struggle.
Yes. *Yes!*
Because he states he didn't really get any breaks. Over there, he does state he's on the vacation he never really got.
(Laughs a little) Yes.
But he's glad...he just wants you to know, he knows that you love him and that he loves you. He just wants you to know and make sure that you understand that you made all the difference in his life.
Oh...he did too!
You know, because as he says, it's like thanks to you, the sun came out.
Same here.
Which makes the loss all the more difficult because, you know, you've thought to yourself, you know, you finally meet this guy and look what happens.
Exactly. Yes!
So he knows you've been frustrated over his passing because you've thought that. Jeez, I finally meet the man of my dreams, so to speak, and then he up and dies!
Yes. There you go!
And you might add to that, life *stinks!*

(*Laughing*) Yes.

And he...At first like when he knew he was going to pass on, there was a feeling of like, now you know, like my life has finally started to buzz and now this has happened. And as he states, he realizes now that he is close, closer to you than he ever was. Even though we relate to things on the physical level.

Uh huh.

But as he says, he realizes that he had fulfilled his life.

Good.

And even though, as he says to me to say to you, even though he did have a very difficult life, he admits that he had a fulfilling life.

Yes. I'd say that.

And he admits he would gladly do it all over again because you'd be at the finish line.

Oh! (*Laugh*) That's nice!

Because as he says, then that would make it all worth it.

That's sweet.

Because he does bless you for bringing joy into his life. And he was glad that many times he was so quick to accept his hardships but realizes now that God does bring joys into our lives as well and you were one of the joys and he's glad that he did willingly accept it.

I feel the same way.

Funny part, he was a very spiritual guy he says. But part of him, like, didn't believe in a hereafter?

Sort of doubtful.

Yeah because he does admit to me that he was on the earth he wavered in his conviction.

Uh huh.

He might have been like "Eh, maybe there is, maybe there isn't. We'll find out when I'm dead."

Exactly!

You know, he wouldn't have rebuffed and said "Oh no, there absolutely is *not*," he would weigh out the pros and cons but then his ultimate, um, logic would be "Well, we'll find out when I'm

dead."
Yes. Sounds like him.
But I have to laugh, 'cause he jokes at me saying he would have thought that I was kind of full of it!
(Laughing) Oh....
He admits he would have definitely viewed me with interest but he would have said, "Oh come on! There's a catch there..."
Uh huh.
Or, you know, there's got to be a way that that's being figured out, so forth. You can't communicate with people who have died. And he's very grateful that he *can* be discerned.
Wow.
Well, he says he can assure you now he's found out there is a hereafter. You *will* see him again someday. Someday he'll welcome *you* into the light...
Oh!
Which he knows is what you look forward to when you complete your life here on the earth. But in the meantime, he does state that...well, he...I've heard this before. He says to me there's only three people on the planet who can communicate with the hereafter. He says, you're speaking to one and he says the other two are out of this area, are out in other continents. But he says 80%, (and I've heard this before from the souls), they say 80% of the so-called phenomena or people who claim they can do it, are full of it!
Wow!
He says there's the 20% that's authentic...
That sounds like him...
And real. And he says the rest of it is just a bunch of baloney.
Yeah. I agree!
Yeah I do too. I like his straightforwardness.
Yes. Oh.
And I'm not accepting that message out of conceit because, of, you know, me being the instrument of this ability, but I basically agree with him. I think, as I said, most of the people that I watch on TV in my opinion, I don't feel they are doing what

they claim they can do.
Yeah?
Well as your boyfriend, as your husband says "Too much is just as bad as too little."
Yeah. That's true.
But again, he admits, he was open-minded, but he would always weigh out the logical.
Yes. Very logical.
He does admit that life had kind of hardened him here.
Yeah.
You know, he had a rough life, he had to struggle, he really didn't get any breaks so he's not going to... as he says, he's not gonna be inclined to believe in Santa Claus.
(Laughing) Neither am I!
You know not when you have, like, a hard life and you see that it's not there.
Yes.
But again, he, even with God, he might have thought "Maybe there is, maybe there isn't." And as he says, "There's no Being over here trafficking us through the universe. It is God is love, God is light. When you come into the light over there, you are in the presence of God."
Is that it?
So it's yes, the energy of those virtues of light and love and it's funny because when they've said that to me, it's interesting because in the Gospel of St. John, John writes, "God is love. God is light."
Isn't that something? They're living the Gospel!
He does admit having a rough time prior to his passing.
Oh yeah.
Because he does bless you for being good to him to the end.
Yeah.
Also in some ways admits he could have been closer to you.
Um...perhaps.
Yeah. He does admit at times he could be a little bit of a tough nut to crack.

Uh huh. Yes.

Yes. But you know typical male. Doesn't want to deal, he tunes out.

(Laughing a little)

You know he just wants you to know, no matter what, he always loved you and knows that you loved him. And hopes that no matter what, you always understand that in spite of any of his moods or pettiness or whatever, there was never any doubt in his mind or should have been in yours, that you loved each other.

Well, that's good. That makes me feel really good.

He admits that he could be a chop breaker.

Sometimes

Yeah, that, you know, he admits that...it's funny because he admits life had caused him to be a little suspicious of trusting again.

Yes.

So, if things started to get too close, he was inclined to almost try to sabotage the relationship.

Could be!

Because he was afraid of being hurt and he had been hurt in the past so this is like a protection. And he admits that there was a lack of trust on his...he had lost a little bit of trust.

Yes. A little jaded.

Because even when he admits the time comes when he passes on, he's ready to let go because he's just kind of tired.

Yes.

Like kind of tired of life, the people here, and the struggle and...

Yeah.

He sees the purpose of it now because he sees now that he did have a fulfilling and accomplished life. But at the time, he really had...didn't see the purpose and wasn't really interested in seeing it.

Yeah. That's exactly right.

So in the hereafter he's gone into the light. He understands the

purpose of his life and he says it makes it all beautiful and worthwhile. But he admits he needed a vacation from here.
Yeah. So do I!
Yeah 'cause he knows you *do* miss him.
Uh huh!
And yet he says he's closer to you than you can imagine. But as he states, sometimes you wish you would pass on.
Uh huh.
But you're not supposed to be there yet.
Darn it!
He says "I can't tell you when, but I can tell you you're not supposed to be here yet."
Is that right?
He says "Because even though you're my sweetheart, you're still your own person and you have your own purpose to fulfill." Right now you'd say to him, "Well, I don't see the purpose."
Uh huh. Sure would.
And he says but you don't sometimes see the forest for the trees, but it doesn't mean they're not there.
They're not there...yeah.
But as he says, when you come here, all will be unveiled to you, where you will see the purpose. Because he says even if you're shown the purpose, like he sees it from his point of view.
Uh huh?
Even if he had seen the purpose of his life when he was on the earth, he either would not have believed it or he would have been, like, "Well, so what? That's not how I feel now."
Right.
He says it's not until you come there that you start to recognize and see the wholesomeness of the purpose.
I see. It becomes very clear.
He says because then it all comes together.
Uh huh.
And you're able to question it and examine it, grow from it, witness it.

Because you certainly do pray for him in your own way.
Uh huh.
Which he does thank you for, asking you to please continue?
I could do more.
He might not have been the prayer type, but he sees the value in it now. He knows what it does.
I'll do more.
He was a man he says who was not into organized religion.
Yes definitely.
I like him already!
(Laughing) I sure did!
And he says but he realizes that there's a big difference between religion and spirituality.
You know, absolutely. I agree.
And it's the spirituality that provides the hope he says, the compassion, the goodness, and the enrichment of your life.
Uh huh. Gee, that sounds so much like him.
Yeah 'cause as he said, you don't have to be, belong to a tribe to be a spiritual person. And I agree with him.
I do too.
I mean I consider myself spiritually Catholic but in the eyes of the Church, I'm a buffet Catholic.
A buffet Catholic. Yeah, take a little here; take a little there.
Yeah and the thing is, you know, they're not happy about that but that's what works for me and…
I'm the same way!
Yeah…and if it doesn't work, you know, if there's a problem after I pass on, well I'll find out then.
Yeah deal with it then. Doing a good job here!
And that's what I say, it certainly is doing me what is….
Interesting though, your husband states that he works with animals in the hereafter.
Oh, does he? He loved them here. *(I enjoyed hearing the "husband" reference so much that I didn't correct him.)*
Yeah 'cause he says he was a people person on the earth and he wasn't.

Uh huh.

And even though certainly he's not being, you know, people boycotting over there, but he's still right now he's so comforted in the presence of the light, he says it just makes it more enhanced when you're with animals.

I agree. Boy!

So he says he works with them over there for now. Even though he says he's still very near to you, because he realizes now that you're somebody that as he always said, you're somebody he could completely love and trust.

Oh.

And there might have always been that little uncertainty, you know maybe about 2%...

Uh huh.

But he's glad to be able to tell you that he *is* with animals in the hereafter and he does talk about pets that passed on. I'm sure, I'm sure he had some in his life...

Oh! Boy. Good.

He states that they're there.

Oh boy. That's wonderful.

Yeah but he did have health troubles, yes?

Yes.

Yeah emotionally and physically.

Yeah.

Because he says he has a rough time prior to his passing healthwise, physically and emotionally. Because he did have physical health trouble, yes?

Yes.

'Cause he speaks of that and he says he also started to take it personally.

Oh yeah.

And that's when it stirred up the emotional.

That's exactly it.

Because it's like, you know, it's almost like in the back of his mind he says he was saying to himself "This is unfair. I'm going to die!"

Uh huh.

You know, "I finally seem like I'm getting something out of life and now I'm going to die!"

Yeah.

He realizes now that it wasn't, um...termination. It was continuation. And again he admits he was a little afraid of death too.

Yeah.

Because he wasn't sure.

I guess none of us are, are we?

Yeah 'cause as he says, now it would be like walking from one room to the next and he could do it all over again easy.

Oh my!

He does say he's walking fine and back to his old self.

Uh huh.

Which would mean...he does admit his balance was thrown off.

Yeah.

From the illness so he states he's walking fine and he's back to his old self in balance. The physical body had the illness not the spiritual. *(Static-like crackling begins here)*

Uh huh.

But you did take care of him?

Some, yes.

Well he does bless you because he says you did take care of him. But he also admits he didn't want to be a burden to himself or anybody else.

Uh huh. Yes. That's exactly how he....

He might have seemed a little cool.

I think so.

And nothing personal. Yeah 'cause the illness sneaks up on him he says?

Yes.

'Cause it's like one day he's, you know, I keep hearing the song from *42nd Street* "I'm Young and Healthy?"

Uh huh

So apparently he was.

Yeah!
And then all of the sudden he's diagnosed with this.
Yeah it's just out of the...
Then he realizes this could be it. *(Crackling lessens)*
Out of the blue.
'Cause he says the illness affected a large part of the body.
Yeah.
You know, even though it's centers in one arena, it's in other parts too but, you know, he might have been complaining about something and was checked and then all of the sudden it's found.
Umm. Sort of.
'Cause he does admit his heart bothered him.
Yeah, it did.
Because at the end he says his heart lurches.
Really?
Yeah 'cause he says his heart fails, which I'm sure it did when he passed on.
Uh huh.
But he said he was having heart trouble.
Pains in his chest.
Yeah, even though that, it's not like he said he's dying of a heart attack but he does say he was having heart trouble. But then a lot of times he thought he was coming down with something.
Uh huh.
Plus he admits he's not the doctor type.
Hmmm. Not really. *(Static again)*
I mean he's not a hypochondriac.
Not exactly, but sometimes he read those medical books! *(Laughing)*
But he's gonna look into it if there's a problem.
Sure.
But he's not going to, you know, lament and dwell on it constantly.
Uh huh. *(Static worse and slight pause)*
Also I heard the name Bill or William. Does that mean anything

at all?
Uh, I know someone who passed with that name.
OK. Because someone just walked into my room and claimed their name was Bill or William. And said to call out to you. But this person's passed on.
Yes.
Oh, ok so it's just somebody that you know.
Yeah.
'Cause he kind of comes as family again but by choice.
A couple of Bills actually.
Well just go with this one, he comes as family but he says by choice. He jokingly calls himself Uncle Bill.
Uncle Bill...*(wondering, perhaps Bill Baldwin who died a few years earlier?)*
But I think it's a term of endearment.
Hmmm.
As he states. Also there's a motherly presence around you too.
Hmmm.
But your folks are still on the earth, yes?
Yeah...
Yeah, 'cause it's not your parents it's grandparents because a motherly presence comes near to you and says she's a grandmother. I'm sure one of your grandmothers has passed.
Uh huh. Both.
So there must be a set of grandparents here but this one claims she's more your mother's side of the family.
OK.
Because she says she knows you better.
Yes. Oh for sure.
And so it's probably, it is the maternal grandmother because she says "I know you, I know you better." You know.
Yes.
Yeah because she says she's met your husband over there.
Oh, *really? (Puzzled)*
Yeah because she says, "We know each other."
Oh isn't that funny.

That they've met up.
Oh...wait! *(Wondering if it is actually Mike's mother Miriam?)*
Also too your husband does state he works with children as well over there.
Does he?
Yeah he kind of more likes the company of small children and animals.
Yeah. That sounds like him.
Just because he finds the whole atmosphere there, you know, it's like somebody on a vacation knowing they never have to go home.
Wow.
So he says he's just taking everything very slowly, comfortably, sorting out his life. You know there's no rush there he says, there's no time.
Wow. Sounds great.
So it's like I've gone to Disney World and I can stay forever! *(Laughing)*
And he says that's why he's...and he says that it's a perfect summer's day here.
Is it? *(Dreary and rainy here)*
He says he looks forward to the day when you come and you and he can share it together.
So do I. *(Sadly)*
You'll both feel like you're on perpetual vacation.
Boy, that will be something to look forward to!
Yeah he says it's something but when you fulfill. He...just with his loss and with your own life you've thought "What's the point?" And he just wants to let you know there is a point.
Uh huh.
(Pause...talks about his cat bringing him a toy in his mouth for play...Several minutes, discussing our cats and how cruel people are to animals.)
But OK, your husband's saying, you know, "Go back to me!"
(Laugh)
Also I heard the name Michael too.

That's his name!

Yeah 'cause he just said "Come back to me, come back to Mike/Michael!"

There you go!

Oh good! And I'm glad I listened. Yeah. But Mike embraces, Michael embraces you with love and also extends the white roses to you in spirituality and the pink roses in love.

Awww. Thank you Mike.

And as he says, he jokes that you talk out loud so you must know he's around.

Oh I sure do! I'm a nut.

So as he says, he's not so far away as you think. You do miss the physical presence, which is understandable. That's what we relate to.

Yeah. For sure.

As he says, when you come here, you'll realize what he's saying that he's a lot closer to you than you can imagine.

Wow.

That he's there and that's why your intuition feels his presence and you start talking to him.

Yes I do. I admit it.

That's he's there.

I've been feeling like a kook, but...

Nah. But as he says, you created such a joyful life for him on the earth, 'cause he didn't come from the happiest family either, he says.

That's true.

You know he just...even like in his love life before you it was always an up and downhill ride.

Uh huh. Oh yeah.

He always felt sooner or later he was being used and he does apologize to you. He regrets the fact that when you did come into his life, he certainly was very happy about it, but sometimes he might have seemed peculiar because it's almost like you had to clean up the mess of past relationships.

Yeah I did feel like the cleanup lady sometimes.

You know, because he regrets it now. He realizes because he was trying...fortunately he had "been through the mill" as he says. He was trying to keep it quiet with himself.
He also admits illness affecting his head?
Yeah.
Because it feels like some big pressure up in my head...
Oh yeah.
He says and the root of the trouble comes from there. *(Static starting again)*
Oh really?
He admits that it affects other parts of the body but the initial problem is like there's a popping in my head. *(Static quite bad)*
Oh gosh yes!
Because he states that when he passes on, it's like he's hemorrhaging..
Oh gosh! Exactly!
In the head, because he tells me there's an eruption in the head...
Yeah!
And, you know, not that it would have made any difference, but it's like they were looking in other places, and yet the trouble was up there. This is what was throwing off his balance, he says weakening the heart. That the pressure was building. Like somebody has an aneurysm. The pressure is building up there and BOINK!
Well...his head was involved in his death.
Yeah 'cause he states that eventually, as he says, that's what causes his passing. 'Cause he says it causes him to go into a sleep state. *(Static still)*
Hmmm.
But he has a health problem in the head, yes?
Uh....
Well no, don't answer that yet! Because it's funny. He says, "If you remember, I said emotional too."
Yeah. Emotional.
That's why I stopped and I...when I realized I questioned you

I said, "No, no, no! Let's stop. Don't answer that." Because he stated…yeah 'cause he admits the blow to the head plays a significant role in his passing?
Oh sure. Yes.
And yet there's emotional pressure up in the head.
At the same time, yeah.
Yeah. Because it feels…'cause at the end he admits he wants to pass on. *(Static)*
It seems that way.
Yeah he's ready to bow out.
Yeah.
It's almost like somebody having a nervous breakdown and not knowing it.
Uh huh. I would say that's part of the problem.
He admits that he had heart trouble physically but he admits he also had heart trouble emotionally. He was sick at heart.
Uh huh! Oh yeah!
And that's the root of his problems he says, in the head and in the heart. Like emotionally in the head and he's sick at heart and that emotional desolation…
Yeah.
Causes the physical. *(Static less)*
Yeah. I think you got it.
As he states that really, toward the end…?
Uh huh…
(Slight pause) **Uh, he's not committing suicide but he wants to die?**
He *did* commit suicide.
You know, but the thing is, I say…he says to me, no he didn't. He did but he didn't. He does take his own life but he's not in the right frame of mind.
Uh huh.
It's not…he's sick at heart.
Sick at heart. Yes. That would be appropriate.
He admits he's suffering an emotional pain…
Uh huh.

And as he says, he didn't judge himself in the hereafter as a suicide...
Really?
Even though he does...'cause he said before he contributed to, like, the ending of his life, which I said that, but then he said to me he didn't commit suicide. And then when you said he did, he's like "No I didn't. Not the way you think."
Oh...
Because the thing is it's...as he says, it's not done as a selfish act.
Right.
It's done as a release from the torment of what he endured...
His heart was broken.
Yeah. He says he's "sick at heart..."
Sick at heart.
And you have no idea what was going through his head. He didn't know what to do anymore.
Oh!
This seems to be the only means of escape.
Poor Mike!
Because as he states, there's other things physically bothering him...
Uh huh.
It's all being set up with emotion.
I see.
That's why before, he mentioned having an illness that spread throughout the body, I started thinking, "Oh did he have cancer?"
Yeah. You *would* think that.
And he thought...it's emotional.
Like emotional cancer.
Spread throughout the body.
In a way...
Yeah. Because he says it spreads throughout the body.
Oh boy. That sounds so much like it.
And he just wants you to make sure you *do* understand that you

did not fail him.
I'm glad to hear that!
He says, "You have not failed me and you have not disappointed me."
Oh really?
"And you have not let me down." Because he says you always were there for him. You did your best to help but he admits your hands were tied.
Yeah, sort of.
He would get into these states. You couldn't make heads or tails.
Uh huh.
And as he further remarks, if he, you know, technically just didn't want to deal, he just didn't deal.
Yeah. Sounds like him.
But he admits he suffered in silence a great deal.
Oh dear.
He shows me the clown costume. He smiled on the outside...
Oh yeah?
But tormented on the inside. *(Slight pause)* **Um, wait a minute. I don't...he showed me drinking also.**
Yeah!
Oh, OK. Because he did admit having a drink problem.
Yes.
And again, this is also medicating him, "Because it makes me feel better," he says.
Oh gosh! You're quoting him.
He says, "It makes me feel better because it takes the edge off."
Exactly.
And yet it's also, on the other hand, bringing the sick at heart anxiety to the surface.
Oh...
And it's also making him more prone to depression or anxiety.
Yeah. Boy, that's always exactly how I looked at it, when it was happening even.
Because he says again about injury to the head.

Yeah.
But, it's like that's the by-product.
Right. The end...
I'm sick at heart
Sick at heart.
And he says it's much like the same thing if somebody's dying from terminal cancer and they're in terrible pain and they end their life, he says it's not a suicide over there.
Is that right?
They *have* taken their own life, but they...they...they...they can see no way out. As he says, the other side works at understanding and compassion not at punishment...
Oh that's good to hear. I was worried about that.
Because he says, "I wasn't sent to Hell."
Good!
And it's funny I suspected it before when he told me he was among mostly animals.
Yeah?
'Cause they'll go there, they'll go to the Hospital of Reflection for therapeutic purposes...
Oh really?
Surrounded only by...it's like a high-class rest home.
Oh neat!
And he said he was with people but kind of like just wanted to...you can tell somebody who's like, recovering.
Is that right? Is it...OK.
That's why he admitted, "I'm glad to be away from here," you know he's being honest but he also recognizes that he was just not in control of himself mentally and emotionally anymore, where killing himself in this manner, it's like, he didn't even know what he was doing.
Is that right?
It's why he states, "It's not suicide." He's not only... he's intoxicated with emotion.
Oh. That's a good term. I like that.
Well that's what he said, he was "intoxicated with emotion."

Intoxicated with emotion.

And...Yeah he admits again that you know, he drank because it made him feel better.

Yeah.

And the thing is he says that's why it *can* be beneficial but it also can be dangerous because then it becomes a dependency.

Boy, that's the truth, isn't it?

And why he says, he didn't realize but...

Now he sees it. Uh huh.

But Christ appears in front of me as the Sacred Heart and says "Peace be with you and peace be with him also."

Oh. Good.

Because you *have* prayed to Christ on his behalf, yes?

Yes.

Yeah because again Jesus appears as the Sacred Heart in spirituality, 'cause I see the Blessed Mother appear as well, as the Immaculate Heart of Mary. So the Sacred Hearts of Jesus and Mary are not here to do a commercial for Catholicism.

(Laughs a little)

But they're coming to ask you if you choose to, to invoke them...

I see.

On his behalf. That you always consecrate him and pray to the Sacred Hearts on his behalf.

OK.

Yeah and again, he says, "Please make sure you understand, you never failed me."

OK.

'Cause he knows you. You'll read between the lines.

Yeah. I'm afraid I do!

He says, "I don't want this conversation to end, this session to end and then you start to..." Because even today you were wondering, would he show up or not?

Oh gosh! Oh sure. I was *so* worried.

You thought to yourself, well...again this is not conjuring, it's discerning. You can't tell me whom you want to hear from.

They have to come on their own.
Exactly!
Otherwise I mean *you* could do it then. But the thing is, as he states, um, that's why he came in first and he kind of like, nudged your grandfather aside like "No, she wants to hear from me. I have the need!" And he had to be a little forceful because as he states, if he wasn't you'd think, "See? He *is* mad at me!"
Yeah. You know that's weird.
Like if we hung up and you said you didn't hear from him and I said, "Well, gee I didn't hear from anybody by that name?"
Uh huh?
You'd think "See? I failed him. He's pissed off!" Or worse you'd think he's like in Hell...
Uh huh. Boy that's just what was running through my mind today!
And that's why he says he rushed in the room and when your grandfather came in he realizes, he's like, "No. Step aside." and that's why he...
That sounds like Mike.
But he's doing it...yes, he's doing it for himself but he's more doing it for you so that you realize that he certainly is near to you.
Well thank you, Mike.
And that you *do* know he's all right and at peace but he's also doing it so that *your* mind can also be all right and at peace. That you can let yourself off the hook, so to speak.
That's good to know. Boy. I've waited a long time for the reading and...
Well 'cause as he says, you never...unfortunately when you do take your own life, even under the most extreme circumstances of not knowing what you're doing, you know, you don't...um, you want to release the people left behind from *their* anxiety that it promotes.
Yeah it sure does do that. A sort of ripple effect.
Yeah and that's why he said trust that what he's saying is to make you feel better and know that he's all right and at peace.

Good.

And again, he's not advocating Catholicism, either but as he says, "If you light candles and pray to the Sacred Hearts of Jesus and Mary on my behalf" he continues to… he's at peace now…

OK.

He continues to be even more at peace. He gets absorbed in even a greater sense of peace and tranquility.

Oh. A higher level so to speak.

Again, it would be like if he had survived this and he was sent to a hospital…

Yeah?

To recover. And he says that's basically what's happened. That there, he's in the Hospital of Reflection with the animals to recover at his own pace and to reflect on his life and understand it. That's why, he again repeats before that, "Yes, in our eyes…yes, but in our eyes, no. He did not commit suicide because, again, he is not in the right frame of mind."

I'm glad to hear that, because that *did* worry me a lot.

I mean, yes, on the death certificate it says you know, suicide, he took his own life.

Uh huh.

Well yes. In human understanding they have no other explanation.

Yeah. That's what we have to say, I guess.

In the spiritual, he says he did…he just was not in the right frame of mind. As he says, "It's like somebody who has much too much to drink and doesn't know what they're doing."

OK.

Oh also too, your husband talks about you moving too.

Uh, been thinking about it.

Yeah, 'cause you're not too long where you are and he just wants to let you know it's all right. He puts covered wagons in front of me to tell you, which would be the evidence of a new beginning.

Oh really?

It's starting to a new direction 'cause, right now, lately, he says you're living your life...you kind of have your life on hold.
Uh huh!
And he says it's time to go into the next chapter.
I agree.
Um, he won't think that you don't love him anymore.
(Slight laugh)
He says he won't think you're being irreverent or forgetful.
Oh no.
But, um, he does want you to be happy and go on with your life because you deserve it and he does regret that in fact at times, yes, you had to put up with a lot with him.
Uh huh. Worth it, though.
He feels the same way. And that's why he states he says, just realize that his passing is not to slap you in the face. His passing is...he's gone over the edge.
OK. That makes me feel way better because I did sort of think that.
Because as he states, emotionally, again, he dies because he's sick at heart.
OK.
Not of anything else. And that the other things are just a by-product.
It's just a by-product.
"Don't feel that you failed me and that this is my statement to you, you know, like I'm going to kick you in the pants or..."
(Laughing)
Because as he says, he just was over the edge at that point.
Over the edge.
And again, the nightmares that were going through his mind. And as the other side says, emotional pain is far worse than physical. Because physical, like, you can possibly *do* something about it.
That's right.
Emotional you can't. You can't take a pill like you can for a headache and you know, make it go away. Emotionally like you

feel down in depression and you can't take a pill and all of the sudden feel like the world is yours.
Yeah. It doesn't work that way, does it?
It's all like that's...(*Long pause as side A of tape ends*)
He...you know did his best. But he still feels in essence that he fulfilled as best as he could with his life. He also admits too that his emotional struggles were genetic.
Oh yeah. That's interesting you bring that up.
Because he says to me that, another reason it's not like your traditional suicide, because he realizes that when he got to the hereafter that there was chemical imbalance in the brain.
Wow. I agree with that.
And as he says, one minute he could be on top of the world and the next minute he's ready to die.
Yep.
But as he says, he discovered in his life review what happens is that the brain is missing a certain chemical.
Right.
To compensate, it overproduces it. And that will make you be very high and up. Then it will wear out, and suddenly plummet down again. Then the brain has to make it again to compensate. And then it's...
A cycle.
A non-ending cycle. And as he says, then you just...you know, after awhile you just can't take it anymore.
Yeah. It's like ups and downs all the time.
You know, being like that, and he says after awhile, he didn't know what to think. Because he says, he could actually, you know, it could be triggered by the slightest thing. Something would upset him and that would trigger the chemical reaction in the brain...
Yeah.
And if there's not enough of the chemical, you know, to keep his balance...that's why he says he's walking fine and his balance was off!
Okay! Well that's good. That's a good analogy.

That his balance is off. But he says once science starts to be able to find out that a lot of illnesses are brain-directed, an imbalance in the brain, especially emotional, he says a lot of people will be able to do away with depression and anxiety.
Oh I hope so! They're terrible.
Yeah that people can go through these things, but...but other than that, he says your life is pretty normal though, yeah?
Hmmm. Not...
I mean I'm sure you have your moments.
Well...it's sort of rough.
But you're dealing with it as best you can.
I'm trying. Yeah.
Because that's what he states. Especially his passing has certainly he knows knocked you on your rear end...
Uh huh.
And turned your world upside down.
Yes it did!
Because as he states he knows that you've been suffering in silence. But...plus people have said the wrong thing at the wrong time.
Sometimes.
Yeah and he says you have to tune it out and realizes that people are asses, as he puts it.
(Laughs)
Yeah 'cause in a lot of ways, he wasn't a people person.
Yeah sort of a loner.
He was, but with reservations.
Uh huh. I would agree with that.
And as he says, 'cause animals don't hurt you.
Yes, that's true.
People will go out of their way to, but he says animals won't.
Animals won't.
'Cause I know you said he loved cats too but he does talk about the cats being there with him.
Oh he called himself...
He says that they're in the rest home, so to speak.

Oh really?
In the place of reflection. Because they're very therapeutic.
He had a real bond with his cats. They were just like people to him
Yeah.
Cat persons, he called them
Absolutely. But as he states, just try your best to pick yourself up, brush yourself off and go on with your life and as he says, don't be afraid or hung up on change or moving, because he does talk about your life. There's a birth in front of you, which in this case is not the real thing. It's symbolic of a new beginning.
Oh. OK. Good. I was getting worried there...!
It would mean going on, like new job, new residence. It's...starting all over again.
OK.
But with a fresh start, which is good, which he says that you need. And he says he won't feel as if you're leaving him behind.
All right. I'll remember that.
But as he states too, just know that he's always with you because he tells me he's gonna pull back now so he can ease...so he can rest more.
OK.
But he's just very...he's thrilled that the Infinite Light gave him this opportunity...
Oh, so am I!
It's great to clear so much up, because he feels he's put your mind and heart at rest.
Certainly has!
Now that's why he says, "Now don't read between the lines!"
I'll try not to!
Take it as the value of what he says, because he says, "No matter what, know that I love you and I'm still very much with you." He says, "You did not fail me," so to keep that in mind.
Oh. OK.
But he says he's pulling back. He has like your grandparents

going back. It's obvious who had the need, who you did want to hear from. *(Laughing)*
(Laughing)
But he embraces you with love in any case as he does call out, 'cause he does call out to family and yet, he's like the "man without a country."
Yes he is.
But he does call out, but you were certainly close to him in his life and still are. And he says, just take care of the animals for us and know that he's there with his pets as well, that he calls out to his family of pets left behind here with you.
Oh OK. I've got one of em.
But as he states, he's very near. But he embraces you with love and he says pray for him as was requested to the Sacred Hearts. But keep in mind, you know, also keep your mind at peace as well. Until we meet again.
OK.
And with that, he signs off and there he goes.
OK.
Well in any case, when you pray for him will you mind keep me in mind?
OK! I certainly will.
And now I'll sign off only because now he *[his kitty]*) **sees me done so he's probably like, "OK! Now you can play?"**
(Laugh)
He's so cute! But in any case, you hang in there and as he says, go on with your life, just know that he's all right. And until you meet again.
OK!
All right. But you all take care.
OK!
Take care.
Thank you *so* much!
Thanks. Bye-bye now.
Bye-bye.

Chapter Seventeen

Life Goes On...

When I put the phone handset back in its cradle I felt giddy with joy and relief. The very air seemed golden and harmonious. I had an irrepressible grin on my face and felt genuinely, 100% happy for the first time since Mike had passed away. I suddenly realized something; I felt *carefree*, as if I had just visited my dear friend in his old bookstore once again! In my heart I had received my "stamp of approval" and Michael had come through like gangbusters, offbeat personality and all. Although March 15, 2001 will fade into the cold mists of time, my belief that Michael appeared in spirit that day will never leave me. I love him for it and appreciate how much effort and preparation it must have required on his part.

The lighter-than-air feeling I got from my session with George Anderson lasted several days and then it settled down into quiet comfort and acceptance. Even though I was convinced Michael had stepped across the veil for a short time, I still missed him. The reading could console me but it could never replace the man himself. I can, however, look forward to that fine summer's day in the future when we shall meet again.

I guess I had come full circle. I had loved Michael. I had lost Michael. But in reality, he had never really left my side. He used to tell me that he would always be there for me, no matter what and I guess he had meant it.

∞∞∞

Bibliography

∞∞∞

Anderson, George, and Barone, Andrew. *Lessons From the Light: Extraordinary Messages of Comfort, and Hope from The Other Side*, New York: G. P. Putnam's Sons, 1999.

Anderson, George, and Barone, Andrew. *Walking in the Garden of Souls,* New York: G. P. Putnam's Sons, 2001.

Breggin, Peter R., M.D. *Toxic Psychiatry,* New York: St. Martin's Press, 1994.

Browne, Sylvia. *Life on the Other Side,* New York: Signet, a division of Penguin Putnam Inc., 2001.

Browne, Sylvia. *The Other Side and Back,* New York: Signet, a division of Penguin Putnam, 2000.

Editors of USA Weekend. *I Never Believed in Ghosts Until...*, Chicago, Illinois: Contemporary Books, 1992.

Edward, John. *One Last Time*, New York: Berkley Books, 1999.

Grant, Robert J. *The Place We Call Home*, Virginia Beach, Virginia: A.R.E. Press, 2000.

Guggenheim, Bill, and Guggenheim, Judy. *Hello from Heaven!* New York: Bantam Books, 1997.

Hill, Aubrey M. *Male Menopause,* Far Hills, New Jersey: New Horizon Press, 1993.

Jamison, Kate Redfield. *Night Falls Fast: Understanding Suicide,* New York: Alfred A. Knopf, 1999.

Montgomery, Ruth. *A World Beyond,* Greenwich, Connecticut: Fawcett Crest Books, 1972.

Moody, Raymond, Ph.D. M.D. *Life After Life,* New York: Bantam Books, 1976.

Puryear, Anne. *Stephen Lives! My Son Stephen: His Life, His Life, Suicide and Afterlife,* New York: Pocket Books, 1997.

Romanowski, Patricia, and Martin, Joel. *Love Beyond Life,* New York: Berkley Books, 1998.

Romanowski, Patricia, and Martin, Joel. *Our Children Forever: George Anderson's Messages from Children on the Other Side,* New York: New York: Berkley Books, 1999.

Romanowski, Patricia, and Martin, Joel and Anderson, George. *We Are Not Forgotten: George Anderson's Messages of Love and Hope from the Other Side,* New York: Berkley Books, 1992.

Romanowski, Patricia, and Martin, Joel and Anderson, George. *We Don't Die: George Anderson's Conversations with the Other Side,* New York: Berkley Books, 1989.

Styron, William. *Darkness Visible: A Memoir of Madness*, New York: Vintage Books, 1992.

Thompson, Tracy. *The Beast: A Journey Through Depression,* New York: G. P. Putnam's Sons, 1995.

Van Praagh, James. *Reaching to Heaven,* New York: Signet, a division of Penguin Putnam Inc., 2000.

Van Praagh, James. *Talking to Heaven,* New York: Signet, a division of Penguin Putnam Inc., 1999.

Acknowledgement

My grateful thanks to famed psychic Mr. George Anderson for his incredible discernment of Michael during our March 15, 2001 phone session. George, you made all the difference in my recovery from some very sad chapters in my life! You gave me inspiration that my dear friend Mike was still close by my side as my "guardian angel."

I extend endless gratitude to my sister Joette who has always been supportive of my creating **A Message from Michael**. With her excellent writing skills and firsthand knowledge of Michael, she helped me polish my manuscript and she kept pushing me to go forward with publishing it on *Amazon*. She's had a very difficult path in this lifetime but she soldiers on. Much love to you, Jo!

I also appreciate support from my brother Bruce Barger, sister Barbara Freeman, sister-in-law Paula Barger and my niece Sara Hall. They met Mike at several parties at my house and they appreciate what a special person he was to me.

I couldn't have made the spiritual progress I have without my dear friend and confidante, Marion Gomes, her daughter Toni Zavolas and grand-daughter Lee Ann Swegle. I also send a big thanks to Marion's niece Maureen Miranda. My longtime friends Karen Hughes Lee and Selene DePackh also have been guiding lights for me over the decades, as have my kind and steadfast friends Bill Barns and Stephen Shelnutt.

I wish to thank the kitties mentioned in this book, because although they have passed on, their loyal little souls continue to bring comfort to me. I believe Mike and Miriam have reunited with them once again and all are happy in The Summer Land! Squeeky, Magic, Stripes, TomTom, Sir Winston, Cassie and Snuggles, please take a bow! And we musn't forget Chuzzlewit. :)

I give a grateful nod to Mike's boyhood friends Pete Seaba, (along with his lovely wife Hazel), Larry Strickler and Dave Prell. They painted a portrait of Michael as an incredible young boy growing up in Sigourney, Iowa.

Through Facebook I became friends with Mike's good buddies Reuben Weaver and Mike O'Harro and I've had the pleasure of reconnecting with John Martzahn (America Online's BeyondVR) and his wife Helen also.

Last but not least I want to thank Mike's remarkable family: His kind brother, Tom Hardesty, mother, Miriam Hardesty Hollowell, his daughters Robin Garrison and Monica Seymour and his wonderful granddaughers, Samantha, Caitlyn, Kelly and Leah and his grandsons Barry and Kyle. Their friendhip over the years has literally been a lifeline in our heartbreaking shared journey of coping with Michael's passing.

The doors that have opened through my association with Mike have been numerous and infinite.

Don't forget, I'll never stop loving you, Michael. Until we meet again...